beyond desert walls

beyond desert walls
essays from prison

ken lamberton

Illustrations by Ken Lamberton

*For Melanie,
who knows
something about
the freedom
of
swallows.

So good to
see you in
Prescott!
Ken Lamberton
4-19-05*

THE UNIVERSITY OF ARIZONA PRESS / TUCSON

The University of Arizona Press
© 2005 Ken Lamberton
All rights reserved
♾ This book is printed on acid-free, archival-quality paper.
Manufactured in the United States of America
10 09 08 07 06 05
6 5 4 3 2 1

Library of Congress Cataloging-in-Publication Data
Lamberton, Ken, 1958–
Beyond desert walls : essays from prison / Ken Lamberton ; illustrations by Ken Lamberton.
p. cm.
ISBN 0-8165-2354-1 (cloth : alk. paper) — ISBN 0-8165-2356-8 (pbk. : alk. paper)
1. Lamberton, Ken, 1958– 2. Prisons—Arizona—Tucson. 3. Prisoners—Arizona—Tucson—Biography.
4. Criminals—Rehabilitation—Arizona—Tucson. 5. Natural history—Arizona—Tucson. 6. Sonoran
Desert. 7. Santa Rita Prison (Tucson, Arizona) I. Title.
HV9481.T83 L357 2004
508.791'092—dc22   2004001862

All illustrations are by the author.

Friendship is a single soul, dwelling in two bodies.

— Aristotle

CONTENTS

ILLUSTRATIONS

ACKNOWLEDGMENTS

Because writing is in part a community activity, I wish to acknowledge those fellow writers, poets, and readers from prison workshops to the University of Arizona Creative Writing programs to my friends in the Rio Nuevo writer's group at Menlo Park. You all have helped me to hone my ideas and to keep my writing honest and clear—any errors that remain are entirely my own. I offer my sincerest appreciation to Al Benz, Lori Biggers, Jennifer Britz, John Buri, Josh Carney, Josh Cohn, Lorna Dries, Dana Doherty, Phoenix Psyche Eagleshadow, Deidre Elliott, Sarah Gage, Steve Gladish, Gordon Grilz, Ralph Hagar, Brook Hardy, Mac Hudson, Madeline Kiser, Dustin Leavitt, Shay Lopez, Tony Luebbermann, Ariel Marks, Greg Martin, Mark Menlove, David Murchison, David Palmer, Julianna Piccillo, Lois Shelton, Melanie Siani, Eliot Sloan, Kiki Thorpe, Spring Ulmer, Scott Walt, Ann Wendland, and Joseph Williams.

A special thanks goes to my writing mentors: Alison Deming, Fenton Johnson, Richard Shelton, Alan Weisman. Your words and friendship continue to have a precious place in me.

To my writing companions John Alcock, Jimmy Baca, Melanie Bishop,

Marcia Bonta, Janice Bowers, Will Clipman, Deb Clow, Greg McNamee, Gary Nabhan, Bob Pyle, Jennifer Schneider, Scott Slovic, Susan Tweit, Ann Zwinger: Thank you for your books and passionate correspondence, which inspired me in the most uninspirational of places and gave me hope.

To my editor at The University of Arizona Press, Patti Hartmann: Thank you for your enthusiasm concerning this book. You are a wonderful encouragement to me.

And for their faithfulness and pain, my deepest gratitude goes to my four blonde cactus flowers: Melissa, Kasondra, Jessica, and Karen. You are as precious as the life you've given me.

Some of the following essays first appeared in various publications and have since undergone revisions. "Desert's Child" debuted in *Cimarron Review* in 1995 and was later adapted as "Stained Hands and Character Flaws" for my first book, *Wilderness and Razor Wire* (Mercury House, 2000). An earlier version of "Ruins" appeared in *Petroglyph* in the fall of 1995, and "Fear of Snakes" in *Snowy Egret* in the spring of 1995. "First Time" was published in *Hanson's Occasional: A Magazine of Literary and Social Interest* in 1991. A short version of "Campo Bonito" called "Buffaloed! Buffalo Bill and the Campo Bonito Mine" appeared in *Tucson Lifestyle* magazine in March 1996, and "Adobe, Hawks, and Shadows" is from *ISLE: Interdisciplinary Studies in Literature and Environment* (Summer 2001).

introduction

In 1986, during the summer of my twenty-eighth year, I abandoned my pregnant wife and two small children for someone half my age. Seven months later, I would be on my way to prison.

Until that summer I had been a predictable, if oblivious, husband and father. I was a successful teacher, having just been named Teacher of the Year by my school district. When I wasn't teaching, I spent my summers working as a program director for a YMCA youth camp near Oracle, Arizona—the same camp where I had met and married my wife Karen. Together, we developed environmental and outdoor programs, trained staff, and supervised an operation involving sixty adults and more than fifteen hundred children over the course of the ten-week season. I considered camp my primary focus. Teaching was what I did in the off-season. I was young, but I had a career, a home in a subdivision, a new

---

Above: Fig beetle *(Cotinus mutabilis)*

family, and some direction in my life. I was unstoppable, invincible, as only youth can make one believe. I could do no wrong.

I felt this way even as I left it all behind—such was the nature of my obsession. The girl was one of my students, whom I had hired to work at camp, and what began with mutual infatuation grew like a tumor into a romance, complete with all the emotional energy of secret letters and clandestine glances and dangerous meetings. We were intoxicated with each other, with the electricity of something forbidden. If I allow it to, that summer still seems as magical to me as the one years earlier when I fell in love with Karen. Sleep was impossible and I was losing weight, but the stars were chiseled from glacial ice and scattered over a desert redolent with the scents of mesquite and mistletoe and newly washed hair. Moonlight spread on the landscape like a rumor—it was not a landscape of charmed hills and quiet arroyos, however, but of fear and desperation. Not of tranquillity but of trembling. For the romance had spread beyond my control. I thought that running away with her would solve everything. We could start a new life together. I was a fool. More than our romance ended with my arrest two weeks after we left Arizona for Aspen, Colorado. I was twenty-seven years old. She was fourteen.

The affair—the crime—would send me to prison for twelve years . . . and change the way I think about myself.

Karen's response to my crime amazes me still. Anyone else would have divorced me. I had humiliated her in public, betrayed her in the worst way a man can betray a woman. I was her husband and I had deserted her and my children for someone younger, too young. But Karen set her feelings aside. Against advice from family and friends, she flew to Aspen to collect me, and found me in the Pitkin County Jail in a state she would later describe as near-catatonic. While I faced bond restrictions and lawyers and indictments, she sold all that we owned, moved to Tucson, and began trying to salvage our relationship by drawing me to our children and the approaching birth of Melissa.

Some have said that Karen is weak for choosing to stay with me, that she's a coward, afraid—like many women in abusive marriages—to stand on her own. People have compared her to women who'd rather suffer quietly than admit failure, women who'd rather question their own selfworth and normalize the indignity than face life alone. They've said this to her, many times, usually after she's spoken of her religious convictions. She no longer talks about where she originally found guidance concerning her role with my unfaithfulness. I think she regrets ever reading about Hosea, an Old Testament prophet commanded by God to return to his adulterous wife, Gomer, and to love her. Religious convictions or no, Karen's motivations stem more from stubbornness than fear. Stubbornness and the need to be in control. These are her words. Divorce was never an option for her—separation, possibly, but not divorce. And certainly not another relationship. She could never do to me what I had done to her. Karen has told me—or warned me—that one reason she's stayed with me is because of her power over me, the power of being right. She's given me other reasons even more base: guilt-free sex. She would have to wait a long time for that.

After I went to prison, Karen enrolled in college to study criminal law. She specialized in legislative histories, concentrating on the law behind my crime. She researched the similar statutes of other states and met with legislators. She spoke at conferences and appeared on local radio and national talk shows. Without arguing against the fact that I was guilty, she began using the law and the media, suggesting that my twelve-year sentence was what the constitution called "Cruel and Unusual Punishment." She eventually—after more than seven years—won my release.

Today Karen regrets the time, money, and effort, the emotional energy she devoted to my post-conviction relief, because my release would be only temporary. Karen no longer believes in the equity of our justice system; she knows it was politics not law that returned me to prison. But I see the nineteen months of freedom as a gift. Prison never allowed me, outside the occasional visits, to be a part of my family, to be a husband again, a father. I had made the decision to return to my wife and daughters shortly after Melissa's birth, just prior to my sentencing, despite my own emotional ruin and the disparate feelings I had for them and for the girl. Karen's gift allowed me not so much a second chance but a way to continue with our lives. It wasn't forgiveness; it was something beyond—and better than—forgiveness. I could be involved with my wife and children again, facing the consequences of what I had done to them. I could support Karen in her new career with a Tucson law firm, keeping house, washing laundry. I could help my daughters with their schoolwork, ride bikes with them, take them fishing.

My temporary release came in 1994 after one of my arresting officers, who no longer worked for the prosecutor's office, approached Karen, expressing his concern about the harshness of my sentence and offering to testify on my behalf if Karen could get us back into the courtroom. Detective Terrance Wesbrock described my case as a thorn in his side from the day it was assigned to him, saying, "I did not want the case, I did not enjoy working the case, nor was I satisfied with the outcome of the case." Somewhat encouraged, Karen sought out lawyers to file a Rule 32, post-conviction relief, that she had started preparing. The Sherick Law Firm agreed to hire her as a paralegal and take me as a client. Superior Court Judge Alan Minker accepted my case, a rare event in itself, listened to two days of court testimony, and then took three months to make his decision. My lawyers used evidence the state had collected to convict me originally, together with new testimony from both arresting officers, to argue for my release. At my resentencing, Judge Minker overturned my conviction, saying it was time for all of us to move on with our lives. He placed me on probation for the remainder of my sentence and allowed me to go home. Unfortunately, the Arizona Court of Appeals did not agree. A year and a half after my prosecutor appealed the decision to free me, three justices ordered my return to prison, reinstating my original twelve-year term, which I wouldn't complete until September 25, 2000. Twice in my life have three men I never saw beaten me senseless. This was the first time. The second time came shortly after I returned to prison. No one, including the appellate court, goes easy on sex offenders.

I wrote the first drafts of all but the last four of these essays from inside a concrete, eight-by-twelve, two-man cell, propped against the wall at the head of my bunk. It's one thing much of these words have in common, the first thing, although the essays in this collection don't necessarily always deal with prison in a direct context. I've already written that book. Prison (and by the term I mean not only the place but its larger significance—prison as it defines me: criminal, failure, outcast of society) plainly leaks onto many of the pages here. There are other places, however, where prison is not so clear, so conscious, but ringing in the background like tinnitus. Even now I occasionally uncover in my writing some new metaphor or irony that exposes me, and every time I'm amazed.

Rick Bass says that he writes to "make stories of order out of elements of disorder." In the same way, I wrote these essays to try to make sense of my place, struggling through words to understand the insanity of my own choosing, to look inside myself and know my passions and my flaws. This kind of insight—if I may claim any insight at all—didn't come in the beginning but slowly evolved as I persisted with writing draft after draft, "to fill up my empty days and nights," as my wife says. In the beginning I wrote to hold on to an intimacy with places that were at the time only memories—places and events, and the people I loved associated with these, that I could sense whenever a familiar scent or sound or sight trespassed those fences. In this, I wrote to discover and to embrace the loss, attempting to preserve all that I knew would change in my absence, and at the same time, to unwittingly punish myself.

My early drafts focused largely on natural history. With my science background and personal experiences, I grew to know the desert well, and I had begun to find success in writing informative articles for nature magazines, profiling individual species and particular locations. I was teaching again. Still, something was missing; my words lacked emotion.

In 1993, more than six years into my sentence, I published an article on the barn swallows that had recently adopted the prison. I had been watching the birds on their seasonal migration for several years, since three tentative pairs arrived to construct their adobe nests under the visitation ramada. Each April, with a rise in temperature and its accompanying insect bloom, the swallows darted in on narrow wings. And every

September they disappeared with the first Pacific cold front. The article profiled the natural history of barn swallows in general, focused on the adaptive significance of colonial breeding versus solitary breeding (from scientific research sent to me by a kind woman at the Tucson Audubon Library), and hypothesized a reason for the birds' continuing presence at the prison (insect availability due to our wastewater treatment practices). I believed the article was one of my best, mostly because it included direct observations over several years, but it was still only information.

Then, in 1997, after my nineteen-month "temporary release," when I came back to the same facility, the barn swallows were the first to greet my return. It was a poignant meeting. I immediately wrote, "Of Swallows and Doing Time," revising the earlier barn swallow article. I wanted to know why I felt so connected with these diminutive, razor-winged birds. Why migrating swallows? The answer came almost as an afterthought at the end of the essay:

> I gauge my life by the swallows. Their nature, like many things in the world, is cyclic; they live inside the regular heartbeat of the land. Ebb and flow, flex and flux, rise and fall. It's a pattern I can live with, one that gives me hope. As long as the swallows come in the spring and go in the fall, come and go and come, I'll feel their rhythm, measuring it out as a change of seasons. This is the source of my hope: the swallows don't only make me feel the weight of time, they cue me to the passage of time. Where ancient peoples raised stones to track equinoxes and solstices, the swallows are my Stonehenge. In a place where clocks and calendars are meaningless, where hours and days and months percolate into one homogeneous, stagnant pond, I mark the swallows.

In subsequent essays, those that would eventually become my first book, *Wilderness and Razor Wire: A Naturalist's Observations from Prison,* I found other profound meanings—toads that tied me to my children, trees that cut holes into the fences, connections to beetles and weeds and whimbrels that I valued more than freedom itself.

I wrote the seeds of the following essays during my early prison years up through the months of my temporary release—before I wrote

Wilderness—so these essays are a kind of prequel to that book. As I looked them over for a possible collection, I saw some of the same meaningful connections, connections to my crime as well as my place, to the people who remained in my life and those who didn't. What's revealed in *Beyond Desert Walls: Essays from Prison* seemingly arose (I believe) through the language itself, as if I had no choice in the matter: a wonderful, deeper, frightening understanding of myself, of a human nature.

Ken Lamberton #61728
Tucson, Arizona

beyond desert walls

desert's child

From the upper bunk where I write, a narrow window allows me a southern exposure of the desert beyond this prison. Saguaro cacti, residents here long before this rude concrete pueblo, fill the upper part of my frame. If I could open the window and reach out across the razed ground, sand traps, and shining perimeter fence, I might touch their fluted sides, their glaucous and waxen skins. But it's enough for now just to see them, standing erect in the distance among the creosote, prickly pear, and paloverde. The saguaro is the literal soul of the Sonoran Desert; its slender columns spell this out, uplifted and arranged like the Greek letter psi. There was a time when I couldn't see this, a time when I looked at saguaros and saw only dark hands with fingers poised in obscene gestures. And I connected with the significance. It was what I admired: an arrogant defiance of this extreme place.

Above: Tarantula *(Aphonopelma chalcodes)*

When I first came to this desert in 1968 as a child, I killed things. Whether spined, scaled, feathered, or furred, they all fell to my slingshot and BB gun. In the desert lot behind my house, I hunted whiptail lizards to near-extirpation, hanging their broken bodies on the spines of a prickly pear cactus as if they were trophies of my budding manhood. Around my neighborhood I stalked songbirds to skin and mount following the directions of a mail-order taxidermy kit. I imagined I was James Ohio Pattie, Daniel Boone of the Southwest, using my skills as a trapper and explorer to survive off the land. But in truth the animals I killed were sacrifices offered up to my own selfish curiosity and ignorance. It had nothing to do with survival. Killing was my way of dealing with an environment I didn't understand, a brutal, arrogant reaction to its incomprehensible and awful strangeness. And because everything was strange, I killed over and over again. It was my first religion.

I paid particular attention to saguaros. At first I did this by using them for targets when throwing rocks, launching spears, or practicing with an archery set. Once, while I was trundling boulders in Pima Canyon, the collision between the opposing energies (kinetic versus potential) of a falling rock and stationary saguaro snapped four feet off the cactus's crown. The break was clean and sharp and exposed a circlet of skeleton wrapped in white, spongy flesh. It reminded me of a zucchini chopped in two. When I took to probing another saguaro with a sharpened stick, someone taught me another way to pay attention to saguaros.

"*What* are you doing there?" the man behind me asked. I tried to hide my sap-bloodied weapon and turned to face my punishment. He had trapped me in his yard. To my surprise, however, he wasn't interested in scolding me and sending me home with burning ears. Instead, he diagrammed a cactus in the dirt (with my stick) and explained the damage I was causing, damage like introducing bacteria into the wounds I had made. It was a good lecture, but it would be awhile before I stopped persecuting saguaros.

As I got older, I began visiting the front range of the Santa Catalina Mountains: Pusch Ridge, Pima Canyon, Finger Rock, Sabino Canyon. Hiking here was intimate and absorbing. I learned the well-traveled trails and then avoided them, choosing instead to bushwhack over *bajadas* and along drainages and scale cliff faces. Each time I returned, I became more attuned to the inconspicuous—the furtive call of a mourning dove in 110 degree heat, the pulse of water constricted by rock. I learned that cicadas, "cold-blooded" insects, love the heat. Their electric whine heralds the approach of the summer monsoon: precisely six weeks following their first song, according to local folklore. I often came across the discarded skins of their larvae shortly after their emergence, the keratinous casings clinging to branches and twigs of mesquite trees like split seedpods. For a few short weeks, the male's monotonous serenade calls females to breed, completing an annual cycle. I loved them for their constancy. They cued me to the rhythms of the desert, and even now I hear their seasonal chorus; my ears fairly ring with it. For me, it is an epiphany, not unlike the advent of our summer thunderstorms.

Returning to the Catalinas again and again always brought new experiences. The familiar defiles and outcrops, the canyons and ridges and peaks offered deeper layers of detail with each trip. I wasn't satisfied only to make an acquaintance with the landscape. I desired romance. Even more, I wanted the kind of relationship where romantic chance encounters would be the interlocking strands of some new and profound ecological vision, where I wasn't a mere observer but a participant, where I was connected and my place made sense.

Not surprisingly, the killing didn't stop. But the killing—actually, I preferred the term "collecting"—did become less meaningless. There was a kind of intimacy within the act. Body parts became my personal tutors. A four-foot pelican wing modeled flight mechanics. A tray of skulls illustrated eating habits. I noticed how the imbricated scales of reptiles matched the same pattern in the feathers of birds. I started keeping more dead things in the freezer. My dresser drawers doubled as museum drawers, socks making room for the skin tubes of snakes and birds, underwear for mammal hides. When friends discovered my taxidermy hobby, they brought me gifts of roadkills, deceased pets, victims of pool drownings. My driver's license was my salvage permit. No still shape in the road got past my scrutiny; I was always looking for new species. I grew fond of certain stretches of road, particularly on night drives, expecting additional specimens for my collections.

I collected pets, too. I set up aquariums for fish, and I built terrariums for snakes and toads. I hatched Gambel's quail in a homemade incubator and trained a red-tailed hawk for hunting. Throughout my high school years, my bedroom was a menagerie. I wanted two of every kind, but unlike Noah, the only freedom I ever gave my animals came by way of their death. I had no ethics, a serious flaw in my desired ecological vision. The desert had opened up to me and taught me about its intricacies, its relationships and dependencies among living things and their nonliving environment. I understood that death was necessary for life, that birth was the beginning of death. I even grasped the importance of sex (years before puberty). I had watched house finches tumble and roll over each other in the dust, screaming with their bird voices, the red-faced males mad with lust, scrabbling for females. I saw how the victor, after driving away its rivals, mounted its prize, flushing its wings and shuddering with heat for that two-second, cloacal "quickie." And then there were the cottontails, furry reproductive perfectionists. The males were nearly as fast, coupling and inseminating in a moment's thumping, finishing with a drunken plop, pleasure dazed. And anyone who has seen lesser long-nosed bats feeding deep within the recesses of a saguaro flower, their elongated snouts perfectly (and erotically) fitting the canal of the bloom, can't miss the coital parallel.

I knew about sex from an early age. I knew it was the essence of existence, of life. Even the insects at my doorstep did it, box elder bugs with their sterns locked together, scuttling around like two beads on a string. But what I didn't know about was how human babies were born. I had asked my mother when I was five after my little sister was born. What she told me I believed. She showed me her scar, a white vertical blaze on her belly. "This is where babies come from," she explained. "When the baby's ready to come out, the doctor cuts you open and the baby is born." For years this made perfect sense to me. It was the way I and my brothers and sister had arrived. The fact that, shortly after this revelation, I had seen the live birth of ten kittens, their perfect cat-forms slipping wet and bloody from the uterus of my pet, didn't bother me. Nor was I confused when I witnessed a deer drop her fawn, wrapped in its amniotic sack, umbilical cord trailing from its mother. People were different. I had seen the evidence. And what better evidence is there than a scar?

I remember when I was eleven or twelve, visiting my friends Mark and Todd Svane at their farm in northern Texas. They told me how babies are born, and I, in turn, explained how they are made. "They come out of their mothers the same way calves come out of cows," they said. I didn't believe them but they didn't believe me either when I insisted that our parents mate like animals. Before the end of that summer, the truth settled into place. My mother hadn't really lied to me. My siblings and I had been born under a surgeon's knife, cesarean section—but she *had* misled me. How convenient for her, those C-sections, at least when it came to answering a child's awkward questions.

My own sex education aside, what I continued to ignore was that I was wrong about many things. I was out of balance. There wasn't any purpose to my desert education. I was taking, and giving nothing back.

Immediately following high school, I went to college to study biology, unavoidably, it seems. This formal education attempted to redefine my background experiences with nature, labeling them and tying them up into neat packages like cuts of beef. But it seemed necessary at the time, this idea of a concrete foundation in science. I benefited from upper-level courses like invertebrate zoology and marine biology. But my favorite classes lacked textbooks altogether. In one class called "Selective Studies in Malacology," the professors outnumbered students. We spent a week together in the mountains of northern Mexico searching for snails. I returned with a tiny boojum tree that I had shoveled from the ground at Punta Cirio, the only place the rare succulent grows on mainland Mexico. Border officials quarantined the boojum, but a fat chuckwalla, hidden under my shirt, escaped detection. This course offered more than knowledge and experience. It offered specimens for my collections, new species to catalogue and file away.

When I married in my senior year, Karen, born and raised in the desert, became the perfect partner for me. She was the assistant curator of my collections, accompanying me to the beaches of Mexico and the mountains of the Southwest. She also had taken lessons in the Catalinas. As we moved from homes to dorm rooms to apartments, she learned to care for fish tanks, birds of prey, and chuckwallas. It wasn't until I finally graduated and settled into teaching that my collections found a purpose outside my own pleasure. Now, everything, my entire life's experiences and all its natural extensions—hobbies, interests, and talents—came to focus on teaching biology. It seemed my life was making sense.

Within a few years of teaching, I had branched out into extracurricular programs that included a science club, which traveled around the state on monthly wilderness expeditions; an after-school taxidermy class; and an annual cooking and eating event we called "the Beast Feast." My collections, caged and displayed in the classroom, attracted much attention. Now my students brought me gifts, both alive and dead—so many, in fact, that I didn't have cages for them all. Some I just let roam free in my room. Jerald, the science department chair, complained about the smells, the loose (lost) creatures, and the potential dangers of rattlesnakes and biting varmints. But he supported me. When another teacher objected to the condition of my refrigerator, he even defended me. "That refrigerator belongs to the science department," he told her. "If you don't want animal hair in your lunch, there's another one in the teachers' lounge." *My* refrigerator got a lot of use. I had packed its freezer compartment with the skins of javelina and deer, owls and snakes, and a menu of donated meats for our wild food feast. When a fellow teacher and hunting friend gave me the whole carcass of a mule deer he had killed, I had to remove the shelves and vegetable crisper to fit it inside while the meat cured. One night an alarmed janitor found a pool of watery body fluids blossoming on the floor. (He probably thought it belonged to one of my belligerent students.) He wasn't happy about cleaning it up, and he let me know about it the next morning. But soon he too was bringing me desert treasures.

Because teaching took Karen and me to another city away from Tucson, our hometown, we traveled a lot the first years. One strip of road along Highway 89 called the Pioneer Parkway was our favorite. The parkway, a botanical reserve with rest stops, monuments, and picnic areas, was less congested and more interesting than the freeways. It was also a grocery store for roadkills.

Training hawks for falconry demanded quantities of fresh meat, preferably with the roughage intact (skin, bone, fur, feathers). Not only did the parkway provide this roadkill cuisine, but it also produced the salvage for my taxidermy students. On the parkway, great horned owls were accustomed to preying on rodents as they skittered across the warm pavement, their cheek pouches stuffed with the seeds of grasses that thrived on the road's margins. Unfortunately, the owls' habits for easy pickings periodically cost them their lives. One night, I found two of them, lying like feather pillows in the road, their bodies warm and eyes bright as though only resting. Whereas other animals usually melded with the asphalt, their broken forms like divots of turf, heavy with death, the owls seemed as though they might take flight at any moment. Driving home with them on the floor of my cab, I wondered what I'd do if one suddenly rose up in life, huge talons slashing at me for freedom.

It was this apparent vitality, even limp in death, that made great horned owls such appealing subjects for taxidermy. One of my students, Jody, became an expert at mounting them. She never complained about the delicate (and messy) flesh removal, but blow drying the owls' thick plumage did try her eighth grade patience. We discovered that a horned owl's feathers outweigh its bones.

At about the time Jody had finished a pair of owls, a local newspaper ran a feature story about my taxidermy class. My students gave the reporter and his photographer quite a performance, scraping hides, shampooing birds, and touching up head mounts, while providing interviews. The article appeared as a full-page spread in the lifestyle section. The publicity pleased me, but I had one concern. The reporter had failed to mention any permit to salvage and preserve wildlife for educational purposes. I didn't have a permit, only a letter from the Game and Fish Department.

That week, the *Associated Press* picked up the article and it went national. I didn't know this. I also didn't know that certain government wildlife agencies had become very interested in my after-school activities. I was in the middle of teaching third period Life Science when two uniformed wildlife officers walked into my room. They were serious. I left my class and followed them to the teachers' area. "We need to see your animals and your permit," the man in the U. S. Fish and Wildlife uniform said. "Okay," I answered. I directed them to my lab area, dug out some paperwork, and opened the freezer. The Fish and Wildlife officer was not happy with my paperwork. "You should have a federal salvage permit," he told me. "You're in possession of federally protected animals." I knew this, and I knew about the need for the permit. I had just neglected to get one. Fortunately, my letter was enough to disappoint them. They gave me a lecture but no citations. After they were gone, the principal of the school told me how they had charged into her office, threatening to arrest me. The whole incident unnerved me; it was the "saguaro lecture" all over again. My behavior hadn't changed.

As a hunter and angler, I had had a few encounters with wildlife officials and other law enforcement people. My falconry activities invariably drew attention, whether I was driving down the road with a hawk on my fist or following a hunting bird onto private property. Once, a police officer stopped me for faulty taillights when I was returning from an evening of dove hunting. He noticed that my hands were soaked with blood and asked if I had injured myself. I should have been embarrassed about this foolish macho tradition of unwashed hands following a hunt. (My hunting partner and best friend, Terry Hutchins, and I always bought cherry Cokes at the same Circle K, blood and feathers sticking to our hands, after cleaning our kill.) The officer checked my limit of birds and my hunting license, and told me to get my lights fixed. He must have thought I was sadistic.

Maybe I was. This business of blood held a measure of fascination for me. My wife thought it was juvenile, but she didn't understand. She had had enough of blood. To her, blood meant weakness and loss and pain: the blood of menstruation, of irretrievable innocence, of childbirth. Blood was personal and private; when confronted with it she always washed her hands. But to me, the pride of life was blood. It was a sign of strength. Blood on my hands, extraneous blood, meant that I was a survivor, that I could dominate my world. I could protect my family and provide flesh for them. Karen preferred to work in her garden among chlorotic vegetables.

It would be a long time before my bloodlust would begin to surrender to a more mature ecological awareness, a conservation ethic. A long time confined to one place. But the desert is patient, and it would eventually lead me, little by little, away from killing (and its antiquated relationship to manhood) to a simple and more profound appreciation of living things. And in this, I could find intimacy. The child of the desert, nursed, weaned, and raised with heat and thirst, thorn and wound, would grow into a naturalist.

This began in prison, where I worked as an education aide, as changes with my teaching. Instead of focusing on the structure of lectures, notes, and books (of which we didn't have much), my teaching took on a more open approach. I discarded the dry, ineffective methodology I had learned in college and used in public school, looking to my fellow inmate students for another structure. Rather than my curious collections and displays, my students became the center of learning. I took a seat next to them, scribbling notes instead of regurgitating facts in the traditional, spoon-feeding teaching style. I looked for ways to teach tangentially. I relied on what I called "teachable moments," gifts from the desert that come by chance, by serendipity. Lesson plans were obsolete here, even sacrilege. In our "prison classroom," we might find a tarantula out prowling for a mate after a storm, or we might get a soaking looking for toads. Both could be lessons. I had to become a teacher's aide to the desert, allowing it to try on my students the same methods it had used on me. I could only master teaching by giving it up.

Outside my window, Gila woodpeckers argue among the saguaros for the best nesting cavities. Their voices, a shrill *huit huit huit,* carry all the way into my cell. The giant cacti, obscene gestures aside, really aren't as defiant as I have said. They, like me, have adapted themselves to this place over time. They've accepted the desert for what it is, on its terms. Their roots, shallow mats of tough rope, radiate out more than fifty feet to take advantage of only a few inches of rain each year. Their storage-jar columns have pleats to maximize water containment when water is available and a thick, waxy cuticle to minimize water loss from evaporation when it's not. The spines, splayed from areoles along each rib, also help conserve moisture by providing shade and creating pockets of insulating air while discouraging thirsty browsers.

But saguaros aren't selfish either. During the driest, hottest, most wicked time of year, the foresummer of May and June just before the monsoon season, the cactus offers sweet refreshment. At a time when many other plants are either dead or dormant, the saguaro bears fruit, its figlike *pitahayas* splitting like chapped lips to ooze a bloody pulp studded with tiny black seeds. It is a boon to wildlife. Curve-billed thrashers and mourning doves relish the feast. What they knock to the ground, coyotes and javelina and tortoises gladly consume. Even the harvester ants will celebrate, single-filing away the nutritious seeds.

By this, the saguaro gives back some of the wealth it has acquired in its kinship with the desert. As part of a larger community, it is only natural. And so, I, too, could do the same. What I have taken I might now give back; what I have learned I could teach. To do otherwise would be arrogant and childish, contrary to the desert's way, my way.

ruins

Red was the color of cold on the Colorado Plateau that March. De Chelly sandstone red. A frigid wind gathered in wavering gusts, sifting plumes of sand, like an atomized powder of blood, in one direction and then another. The hue suffused everything: our clothing, hair, skin. Even my mouth carried grit from that frozen, dust-redolent desert.

I complained about my lack of clothing, but Terry Hutchins, my teaching colleague and hiking *compadre,* said I'd be all right. "Once the sun's up and you're climbing," he assured me, "a sweatshirt will be enough. And there's less wind in the canyons." I wasn't so sure. But after driving in the dark for an hour, with the ghostly shapes of saltbushes jumping up in our headlights and then vanishing as we crossed a trackless section of Navajo reservation, I was committed. And so we entered Monument Valley via the trail to Hunts Mesa.

We traveled with two of Terry's friends, Chuck and Annie LaRue. At

Above: Anasazi pots

the time, Chuck was an environmental scientist with Peabody Coal Company, a mining outfit of roaring, sauropodlike power shovels and miles of roads, conveyors, railways, and slurry lines that extracted bituminous coal from reservation land at nearby Black Mesa. As a concession to the Navajo and Hopi people, the company paid Chuck to monitor the strip-mining impacts and then help return the mesa to some semblance of their pastureland afterward. He was an expert naturalist, raised and educated locally, having attended the reservation's Bureau of Indian Affairs (BIA) schools (although neither he nor Annie are Native American) and then Northern Arizona University. We were there in that naked place of natural arches, sandstone monoliths, and Indian ruins because Chuck wanted us to see where a B-52 bomber had crashed the previous October. I had come, somewhat reluctantly, to experience only the land; I had seen enough of exploded aircraft.

Chuck's explorations in the area had uncovered marvelous treasures. Following his directions, on our drive up to Kayenta the day before, Terry and I had located the fossilized tracks of Dilophosaurus, a twenty-five-foot, carnivorous, Triassic Period dinosaur—called a theropod—that had once hunted among the cycads and tree ferns of a floodplain now turned to sand and bentonite clay. The tracks we found wouldn't fit inside a hubcap, and there were pathways with hundreds of them, each one with toes and claws like the foot of a giant bird. Chuck also knew where 180-million-year-old teeth from extinct, thirty-foot, crocodilelike phytosaurs lay scattered on the ground like pottery sherds. He'd held palm-sized skull fragments of armored shovelheads or motoposaurs from the Cretaceous, and he'd found amphibian tracks in Permian sandstone. The night before, he had talked about these places, their names embodying their enigma: Skeleton Mesa, Spearhead Mesa, Owl Rock, Cutfoot Wash, House of Hands Cave. And then he handed me some photographs he'd taken recently. Partly hidden in a cleft of rock, three large round clay pots with black and white wave designs waited for their owner to return. They could have been placed there yesterday. "They're called *ollas,*" he said. "They've been in that cave more than seven hundred years. And I left them there."

We left the truck as gray rocks and sand began to redden with the dawn. A dry arroyo led us between high walls of sandstone, and we had to step among blotches of snow where shadows have prevailed for eons. I hiked along the floor of the narrow canyon toward Hunts Mesa with the images of clay pots fixed on my retinas. I wondered about their significance, and my own insignificance in comparison. Seven hundred years. Somewhere out there—Chuck wouldn't say where—relics of a mysterious people still tell a story to no one but rocks and sand and lizards. I found myself wanting to know more about them. Who left their fingerprints pressed into the coils of those globes and painted their culture onto their burnished surfaces? Who carried them to that cave and left them there? For what purpose? More than all the deserted ruins and empty granaries I would touch in that place, those three clay containers held the absence I was feeling all around me.

I had heard about the Anasazi, a desert people who appeared in the Four Corners region more than two thousand years ago. The name is a Navajo word variously translated as "Ancient Ones," "Someone's Ancestors," "Enemy Ancestors," "Ancient Enemies," or "Old Strangers," depending on the romantic inclinations of the translator. In the beginning, the Anasazi were basket makers who lived under overhanging cliffs and in caves, gathered wild plants, and hunted small game with atlatls, a special stick for launching spears. Later, they became more agrarian, giving up their nomadic life and their baskets for more durable pottery, shifting toward urbanization, moving into clusters of pit houses while supplementing their diet with corn, squash, and beans: the Holy Trinity of Native diet. Their agriculture flourished. Diversion dams and fields terraced on alluvial fans near side canyons allowed them to plant more crops. More crops meant more people. As their population grew, Anasazi culture began influencing other peoples, spreading across the region into an area roughly the size of Arizona. They replaced pit houses with surface dwellings with upright, mortared sandstone walls. Pottery for both everyday and ceremonial use became more imaginative, displaying aesthetic designs with geometric patterns. Cotton weaving produced more practical and comfortable clothing. And trade brought in valuable commodities such as sea shells, obsidian, and parrot feathers. They had elaborate road systems, line-of-sight communication towers, and irrigation canals with catch basins, reservoirs, and dikes built into arroyos to store and channel water into fields and towns. By A.D. 1100, the Anasazi were the Southwest's most dominant and sophisticated people. But those three clay pots, hidden in an inaccessible cliff face, speak of a later time, one of puzzling cultural decline and abandonment.

We hiked awhile before Chuck and Annie outpaced us and disappeared into the canyon. They'd been there many times, but for them the bomber wreckage was new. I told Terry about a recurring dream I'd been having of dying in an airplane crash:

I'm nineteen years old and my father is with me. He's wearing his Air Force flight suit, the same one he wears in the photograph I have at home. We're going somewhere important, but I don't know where. He seems pleased to have me along and says it's been too long since we last had time together alone. It's weird but even as he speaks to me, I know he's been dead for ten years. Anyway, he gives me the window seat. On takeoff, the plane rolls over and I see the ground coming toward me. Next, I'm standing over our bodies, burnt and twisted into the wreckage. Then I wake up.

Terry thought I should see a shrink. And maybe travel by train.

Where the canyon broadened into full sun Chuck and Annie waited for us. We scaled a steep hill of sand that crept out of the mesa like grain leaking from a ruptured silo. The fine sand pulled at our boots, drawing us downslope. Without firm footing we had to take three times as many steps to cover the distance. Behind us the sand slipped away in sheets like rolling liquid, gathering momentum and cascading downward in miniature cayenne tsunamis. In the Permian Period 250 million years ago, when the world was one supercontinent called Pangaea, immense seas of sand drifted across northern Arizona and eventually became cemented into eolian or wind-deposited sandstone. We'd already seen them: lithified sand dunes with visible and unmistakable lines of crossbedding. Once lifted and exposed, however, the sandstone slowly erodes, transforming back into boot-sucking grains in a cycle that endlessly repeats itself.

From the crest of the hill, a little valley opened northward, bordered by high, uneven sandstone walls on the left and rising hills on the right. Dwarf piñon pine and juniper speckled the hills and outlined every naked dome and escarpment of protruding rock. We stood at the broken feet of Hunts Mesa. A stock trail directed us along the floor of the valley. The walking was easy. A touch of breeze chilled the back of my neck and spine, dabbing up the moisture of my earlier exertions. The temperature was perfect for strenuous hiking in sweatshirt and jeans, the sun warm and bright.

Ahead, a flock of dark-eyed juncos played hopscotch with us, skipping down the trail in pairs and triplets whenever we got too close, uncluttering the ground like leaves in a gust of wind. I enjoyed the game, the freedom of its simplicity. We got closer to the birds each time, and I wondered if they weren't having fun too. With every bolt, they flared their tails, unveiling a flash of white feathers. Their tiny wings sputtered with a sound like burning sapwood.

Farther up the valley, we hiked along alluvial terraces beneath sun-glazed cliffs. Darker, liver-colored draperies of desert varnish, a mineral wash of iron and manganese, percolated through the porous sandstone and stained the walls in trickling liquid patterns. In places, whole sections of the cliff unscrolled into narrow side canyons, potent with color and the sensuality of water-worn sandstone. There, Chuck pointed toward a small natural hole near the rim of a high wall. "Sphincter Arch," he said, and we laughed at his label. He then challenged us to find the ruins. "Ruins?" I said, searching the length of the wall. I didn't see anything but sandstone and shadows . . . and then I found them, tucked into a broken cleft just above some terraces, blending perfectly with the surrounding rock. As we climbed to them, details in their structure materialized: a hidden doorway, slotted windows, and walls of rectangular stone slabs laid in adobe mortar. Foot- and handholds, chiseled into the cliff but really only large enough for toes and fingertips, allowed us access to the cleft. Inside, the air smelled like mummy dust. Warmth radiated from stone heated by the morning sun and felt like a balm against my cold-stiffened skin. *I could give up teaching and live here,* I thought. *Begin my hermit fantasy, abandon the world and its machines and become untamed in these canyons.*

The ruins were mostly intact, undamaged by time and weather and gravity, except for their ceilings. *I'll replace the juniper logs, overlay them with brush and grass and tie it all together with plant fibers using square knots.* The Anasazi always used square knots. It might have worked. The natural stone recess would continue to protect the three small rooms for a few more centuries, much longer than I would need them. I might have lived with the dirt and hair, gathered wild food—piñon nuts, black and red currants—planted a few native crops. But what would my wife have thought? I was too old, already too urbanized and domesticated for hermithood.

I stuck my head through the doorway of the smallest room. It was dark and now the smell took on a sharp odor of urine. As my eyes adjusted, I saw the room's purpose: a granary. Among the scattered sticks, clods of dirt, and other wood rat–gathered refuse, a pile of dried corncobs covered the floor. I reached in and picked one up. The coffee-colored cob was the size of my thumb, but it still resembled our modern hybridized corn, even with the tiny kernels missing. Chuck told me that the cob I held was left behind after the Anasazi inexplicably fled these canyons around A.D. 1300. "They left everything—homes, fields, fully-stocked granaries."

I'd read about the theories—war, drought, soil degradation, or combinations of the three, beginning about the middle of the twelfth century. Displaced Anasazi retreated into huge communities like those at Mesa Verde, Canyon de Chelly, and Kiet Siel Canyon. There they constructed some of the most spectacular cliff dwellings, probably as protection against marauding tribes or even their own Anasazi neighbors, as resources dwindled. It was a futile effort, though, for in little more than a century, the cliff dwellers had abandoned these too.

Chuck thought that our ruin was a vestige of one of the small settlements common in Monument Valley during a population dispersal between A.D. 1250 and 1300. Perhaps, he said, they cut too many trees for firewood, erosion resulted, and the desert could no longer support their large numbers. But where did these people go? I wondered. Did the Anasazi become today's Pueblo Indians, like the Zuni and Hopitu, as many archeologists believe? The Hopitu still live in northern Arizona, still construct mud and stone homes on nearby mesas. Even their pottery has similarities to that of the Anasazi. Maybe the Anasazi never really left. Maybe all the lost ruins and pottery indicate that these people simply moved and found a better life. Hopitu means "peaceful people." We call them "Hopi," but the name sounds like hope.

We climbed into a defile south of Hunts Mesa. Rabbitbrush, saltbushes, and bone-white grasses tied together a thin juniper-piñon woodland. The mealy-leaved saltbushes seem to prefer the alkaline soil, colonizing places other plants cannot, particularly the salty, undrained sinks of the Great Basin Desert.

But rocks were still the prominent features there, and we had to mount a gigantic staircase. My excitement grew as Terry and I approached the mesa top. Chuck and Annie, once again out of sight, had told us about a dramatic overlook into Monument Valley where the trail leveled at the western edge of the mesa. The overlook was close to the place where the B-52 Stratofortress, one of two bombers on a night mission from Fairchild Air Force Base in Spokane, Washington, made first contact with the ground. From there, we would follow where the aircraft had skipped over the plateau and dropped an engine before crashing onto the eastern rim. We'd trace a half-mile path strewn with gears, electronics, and twisted pieces of metal and plastic.

Patches of snow decorated the ground between the slickrock. Juniper and piñon looked swept and stunted, bonsaied by wind. Naked branches littered the trees. Deadfall limbs, some sheathed in snow and others sand-weathered to a satin smoothness, slowly gave back their minerals to a patina of soil. We trudged over ground that sloped away from us. And then suddenly the entire landscape dropped away into sky.

Breathing seemed unimportant. Monument Valley overwhelmed my senses; the perspective threatened to steal my equilibrium, unbalance me permanently. I stood on a shore a thousand feet above a vast inland sea drained of its contents. Distance and space replaced the substance of rock and sand, exposing abysmal roots. Mere chains of islands had become columns and fins, turrets and castles and needles, rising from an unoceaned seabed. Sweeping obliques and verticals, stratigraphic steps cut by wind and rain, gravity and time, extended to and filled all horizons. And with these forms were infinite shades of color. Dark, angular shadows spilled over and penetrated rich limonite-yellows and iron-reds in shifting bands and waves—patterns, I immediately recognized, like those of the Anasazi. I stared into a vast, unfinished gallery, animated with light and color and texture, bent under its own weight into the curvature of the earth.

We broke for lunch at the edge of the world.

A clutch of oval piñon cones crunched like eggshells when I sat down on them. The sound dropped into the windless void. Under a sky the color and hardness of azurite, I peeled an orange, its aerosol hanging around my face, tickling my nose.

When Terry joined me, I told him that I had never really known my father, that I knew more about these seven-hundred-year-old cliff-dwelling strangers than I did about the man who supplied half my DNA. I did know that he was a major in the Air Force, that he flew fighter aircraft (painted in camouflage greens and browns, I remember, because we painted our Volkswagen beetle the same way) as the Vietnam War escalated during the sixties, and that he was the first pilot to fly an F-102 fighter nonstop across the Pacific Ocean from Travis Air Force Base, California, to Naha Air Base, Okinawa, refueling in the air. "This historic flight directly contributed to the successful deployment of an entire Air Defense Command unit on a 7,000-mile mission while maintaining its full combat potential," his citation reads. After his death, I found three steel canisters holding 8-mm films of the flight, movies taken from his cockpit camera showing the slow descent of a cone-nozzled hose from a tanker-converted B-29 bomber. I watched those silent, monotonous films over and over, catching occasional glimpses of his helmeted shadow as it moved across the canopy. I knew that he was a man of professional competence, aerial skill, and devotion to duty because his citations and medals say so, but my memories of him are still only photographs, a few black and white four-by-fives that over the years have reinforced in me the belief that he was real.

Halfway across the mesa we found one of the bomber's eight turbofan engines. Misshapen and dented, it lay in a trough of sand like a beached whale. Other aircraft parts cluttered the area, mostly bits of metal. Terry lifted an ashtray-sized gear and kept the artifact for a souvenir pencil holder/paperweight.

"It was snowing that night," Chuck said, recalling a newspaper account and adding scenes to my own mental pictures and unwanted memories. "The bomber was flying a low-level mission when the terrain-avoiding radar malfunctioned. After the plane's wing tip struck a small projection of the mesa, dropping this engine here, all but the commander of the crew ejected. Their chutes barely had time to open. The gunner died when his didn't."

"What happened to the commander?" Terry asked the obvious.

"He didn't have an ejection seat. He went down with the plane."

On the eastern rim of the mesa something had torn a ragged V from the ground at our feet. Below us, where the mesa steps down onto a broad tread before dropping over a sheer cliff, what remained of that something lay splashed over a half-acre of baked adobe. The area was devastated— plowed earth, charred trees, scorched rocks, and wreckage. The impact had crushed a scrap yard of metalwork against two blackened boulders, jutting from the edge of the mesa like a pair of spatulate teeth. It was like my dream.

Chuck, Terry, and Annie scrambled down to examine the remains. I stayed behind. I couldn't help but superimpose the smoldering wreckage of my dream onto that scene. Only there were no bodies.

And then other memories came. I'm on the mall at the University of Arizona, eating lunch between classes, when the dark, noiseless silhouette of an A-7D Corsair II flies low over the campus. Too low, I think. Its engines have failed, and the pilot is attempting to glide the aircraft to the air base at Davis Monthan. He doesn't make it. He ejects over Arizona Stadium five seconds before his plane rips a furrow down Highland Avenue and disintegrates into a breaking wave of fire. Two sisters, students at the university on their way to class, burn to death after the plane collides with their car. The military awards a medal to the pilot, Captain Frederick L. Ashler, who narrowly missed dropping his aircraft into a crowded school yard.

I've always imagined this was the way my father's plane went down a few days after my ninth birthday. A streaking plume of fire and very little wreckage. The date is imprinted on me: November 14, 1967. His F-105 fighter crashed during an exercise on a military gunnery range near Salina, Kansas, where he was practicing aerial maneuvers prior to his scheduled tour in Vietnam. I was told he went into a dive and never pulled out of it. He didn't eject. He went down with the plane. I remember coming home from school that day, excited about the weekend. It's cloudy, and the wind blows fall's dead sycamore leaves around me; they're tiny hands waving good-bye. A dark blue military vehicle is parked in front of our house. My mother meets me at the door. Someone in uniform waits in the kitchen. She helps me out of my jacket, takes me to my room, and sits me down on my bed. I notice she's been crying. "Your daddy won't be coming home anymore," she says. "His plane crashed. He was killed today." I don't really believe her until I see the wreckage of his plane on the news that night. It, too, is splashed over a half-acre of plowed earth.

After we moved to Tucson and a fog of long, empty months had begun to lift, I found a newspaper clipping between the pages of our family Bible where my mother had slipped it. When I saw the date and realized what it was, I replaced the clipping and turned the page. I couldn't read it. I feared being discovered, of breaking the silence surrounding that day of death—and the thousands of wounded hours that followed it. These were painful details kept hidden. At the time, no one discussed them. I even lied to my classmates and friends about my missing father, inventing excuses for why he was never home. I've looked for that article since then, carefully leafing through each thin page of the leather-bound book, but I can't find it. And my mother doesn't remember ever seeing it.

An acrid smell reminded me of what Chuck had said about the aircraft refueling shortly before crashing. That whole dark corner of Arizona must have flared up on that stormy night. I recognized sections of fuselage. A maze of wire and cable, its insulation seared and crumbling, stretched among the sections like blackened spaghetti. The rest was an unidentifiable conglomerate of metal, bits and pieces, melted and shredded. When I lifted a chunk of electronics forged into a hardened resinous mass, Terry called me over to the edge. Fighting waves of weakness that surged from ankles to groin, I peered over the side. Far below, larger aircraft parts had escaped the fiery explosion on the rim. I noted most of one wing and two landing gears, splayed like a pair of discarded shoes.

Later, after my mind had dulled the edge of the scene on the rim, I noticed that grasses had begun to recover around the site, pushing up bright new needles through metal and plastic. And some of the piñon trees, through their blackened, skeletal fretwork, were showing green. The wreckage had already started to blend into the rocks and sand. As we walked away, I realized that I could forgive this unnatural ravaging of Hunts Mesa, this relic of my culture, this machine and the wound it had caused. Wounds heal, and although they may leave scars on the landscape, we no longer feel the pain—unless we pick at them. The pain of remembering, like a quick flare of light in the silence and darkness, can be left behind. I had begun to understand something new, a kind of truth: the ruins of our modern, space-age world—and maybe even the sometimes tragic burden the debris lays on us—can be abandoned, too. We can leave them behind for something better, as the Anasazi left those simple mud and stone buildings . . . and those three hopeful clay pots.

———————————

On the way back, we ventured into one of the side canyons to see a rare double arch. Cliffs towered above us, squeezing the sky into a ribbon of blue and stretching shadows into pools that enveloped residual daylight. Twilight emerged in the late afternoon. Deep into the canyon's entrails, snowmelt collected in a string of stone basins like an ellipsis at the end of a slickrock sentence. Water mirrored every undulation and hue; pools became windows into an upside-down world of rockbound corridors, chutes, joints, and slots. Mineral crystals rimmed a basin at high water where I stooped to drink. The water tasted stone cold.

A half mile into the canyon, we scuttled on hands and feet to gain a rimrock alcove. Twin vaults of orange rock spanned a slip of sky. The delicate tracery melted gracefully into the construction of the canyon. I wasn't surprised the arches were there. Somehow they fit, like the cliff-swallow homes of the Anasazi that we always seemed to find near arches. I relaxed in a cradle of sandstone, mesmerized by walls that darkened from buff to burgundy, a leisurely mutation synchronized by ebbing sunlight. Seven centuries ago an Anasazi farmer may have rested on that same stone, watching a similar sandstone sunset. I could almost believe he was still there, still growing maize on alluvial terraces and storing it in rimrock granaries. Certainly his spirit, like the stone dwellings and clay pottery, never left those canyons. In that wild place I could sense his presence, as I felt the presence of my father inside me. I know this: It was a fitting place to meet the dead.

monsoon

It was 105 and the humidity was approaching saturation. Physical comfort was a memory from the days before our swamp cooler failed. Clothing soured in less than a day. My hair needed cutting. Dust clung to my skin and, mixed with sweat, formed dark blotches on my arms and legs. The foresummer of that June was miserable. How my wife managed it nine months pregnant, I don't know.

Tucked into the Santa Catalina Mountains' northern foothills, where the desert claws up against grassland, the Triangle Y Ranch Camp had been our summer home since Karen and I had married there in 1981. It was a place of horses and cattle, barbed wire and eroded trails and abandoned mines. Instead of pines, we had catclaw and twisted mesquite, prickly pear cactus with flowers of yellow tissue, and trees appropriately called hackberry. Instead of clear lakes and streams marking grassy meadows, our dry arroyos and algae-clotted cattle ponds cut into hills of baked dust. Overhead, the sun was the color of afterbirth.

Above: Jimsonweed seedpod *(Datura meteloides)*

Karen was the center of attention that summer of 1983. I thought it might have had something to do with her gravid state, and it may have to some degree, but there were other reasons. Karen was personable and approachable. The staff we were supervising admired her, laughed at her sarcastic humor, and appreciated her for her work as special programs director, substitute nurse and counselor, even chauffeur. She often ran errands squeezed behind the steering wheel of the camp truck, bouncing for miles over rutted back roads to transport people and supplies to more remote camping places like the Outpost, Campo Bonito, and Peppersauce Canyon. (After the camp director won the birth-date pool, I heard rumors that he had sent her on a particularly rough delivery near the day he picked. Tom missed the exact time of birth by twenty minutes.)

Four summers earlier Karen and I had met at this YMCA youth camp. I was twenty and director of the backpacking program; she was a seventeen-year-old counselor. I fell in love with her late one night at her cabin when we were supposed to be planning our next backpacking trip. It could have happened to anyone, I suppose, given the circumstances. We were both exhausted from a ten-mile reconnaissance hike that day. A single candle lit her cabin, and her bunk was the only place to sit comfortably. We were alone. When she kissed me (and then told me I'd better leave), I knew I was in for it. No one had ever kissed me like that, with that mixture of passion and vulnerability. Karen actually *wanted* me! That night I walked back to my cabin under palpable stars, believing that the past few years of disappointing dating and failed romances had ended. No longer would I have to suffer the emotional swings that stalked me into every one-sided affair since my first crash-and-burn at fourteen. Karen would relieve me of my obsessive tendencies in my relationships with women; she afforded me a kind of emotional security. I could feel free with her—reason enough for me to pursue her.

For Karen, emotional security and her relationship with me stood on opposite poles. I had awakened feelings within her that, previous to our meeting, she was either unaware of or had repressed. She had just emerged from childhood. I was her first love, and it had caught her before she understood its power and its danger, its lightning strike of ecstasy and return stroke of pain. Today, a much wiser woman, she wishes she had explored her passions more and been done with it. "The worst that could have happened," she's told me, "was being stuck with one baby to raise alone instead of three." Her conservative Baptist grounding, however, taught her that her feelings meant only one thing—marriage.

We married in the camp chapel eighteen months after we met, still the only marriage performed in that open stone-and-wood structure.

Now we were about to have our first child. Marriage was shifting to *family,* freedom to responsibility. Nine months before, straight out of college, I had accepted a teaching position in Mesa, Arizona, a hundred miles from our home in Tucson. The transition was hard for both of us, but more so for Karen. We had no place to live, so we stayed with my friends, Jeff Teich and Terry Hutchins, camped out in their Tempe apartment in our dome tent on their living room floor, while the bank approved the loan for our new home. I liked our living arrangements. I was among my friends, a package Karen had accepted with our marriage. For me it seemed like being back in college, living on campus in a dorm, a lifestyle I missed. Only now, work substituted for school and I never had to deal with finding a date. I didn't need anything; Karen cooked my meals and washed my laundry. I didn't even mind sharing her with the guys. I was proud, actually, of her ability to keep the apartment for me and the other men. We were partners, pouring resources into each other as we confronted the challenges of our new life together. We had a perfect marriage.

Karen hated those months. I never knew it—I never asked—until she told me years later. We had no privacy, but what bothered her most was my insensitivity to her need for privacy. My ignorance frustrated her; that, and the feeling of being trapped in a bad situation where complaints were useless. I wasn't listening. She's told me since then that she should have slept with my friends, that maybe *that* would've gotten my attention. It would have. I was shocked when she suggested it, and for the first time, I realized how serious she felt. My excuse was that we had no other choice. But Karen would have preferred camping in the desert without running water over camping in someone else's apartment.

Karen conceived in the fall when we managed to get away for a weekend. We had my mother's house to ourselves, her pool and Jacuzzi. The water was hot and excited and so were we. What began as fooling around under turbulent bubbles led to a desperate struggle to pull off our wet swimsuits under damp sheets. Karen warned me what would happen. We'll make a baby, she said. And we did. A month later she was throwing up every time Terry made his morning toast. The guys at the apartment began calling her "Prego."

It was so hot and sticky that summer at camp that clothes were a burden. I couldn't imagine how Karen dealt with the extra weight, carrying the baby. She was in her sixth month when she crossed the 100-pound threshold; never before had she weighed that much. Now she was 130 and obvious. But Karen was so comfortable with the idea of having a baby that she didn't even sweat in the heat. Motherhood was changing her, physically and emotionally. Even her thinking was different. It was as though her pregnancy had altered her whole person, preparing her for some mysterious end as her belly grew. I, however, remained the same. I couldn't understand it, so I ignored it. Denial was easier; nothing would change.

As home got more unbearable I went looking for rain. It would come soon, I knew. That's the way it worked in the desert. First would come the heat, and the desiccating winds that shriveled and mummified everything green, sending grasses and wildflowers to seed under a white blanket of incandescence. Then, a subtle change would occur: a rise in humidity as the Southwest sucked in moist air from the Gulf of Mexico. Monsoon winds. Soon, pregnant clouds would appear over the mountains as this wet Gulf air rose above them. Then—rain, great black columns of rain as the clouds would lose hold of their burden. Heat would be memory, and the desert would fill with the sound of trilling insects and toads, greening again in a matter of days. The clouds, those precursors to the monsoon storms and promised relief from the drought, those harbingers of menace and life, were what I went looking for. As sure as Karen's labor, they would come.

Every afternoon that last week of June I climbed the hill behind our residence. But the mountain peaks remained clear, shimmering in defiance of change. Foolishness, I thought, not knowing how much like me they were. I never cared for change. Didn't like its challenge to my complacency. Nearly a decade of high school and college had kept me secure in a world of risk-free choices and parental financial bailouts. And now my marriage was in transition; it no longer fit into my lifestyle ideal. My grip had relaxed and bachelorhood had begun slipping into an irretrievable past, blurred by marriage and now erased by fatherhood. I was becoming Tom, the camp director. We used to fish together, the two of us four-wheeling into the wilderness in search of some remote, untested stream. And then, in a single fishing season it seemed, Tom and his wife had a baby and the four-wheel-drive was gone. I remember the contradiction I felt the first time Tom hooked up his bass boat to the station wagon.

Karen's pregnancy meant a station wagon was in my future, too. I could almost smell the child-proof upholstery, which brought back scenes from my own childhood: images of me, "the oldest," with my three younger brothers and little sister, packed into that blue Chrysler wagon on family outings. I could see my brothers' faces, wide-eyed with pleasure, pressed to the greasy windows, and my own face hidden in the background, afraid someone would recognize me. I hated those trips. I hated the parade as we all filed into Bob's Big Boy and found seating for seven, with me leading the way and feeling humiliated as people watched and chewed their food. Now, I was cycling back to what I never knew then had appalled me—family, the threat to my independence. *Only this time I was planting the seeds.* Family threatened not only my independence but my youth. Family limited my virility, as raising children sapped my strength and resources, drawing me toward impotence, weight gain, and baldness. I had married Karen to escape my emotions, and marriage had led me straight into what I feared most: getting old. I had planted the seeds. And I would be driving the station wagon.

On the 29th of June the rains came. I waited as the clouds bloomed above the mountains, brilliant white masses pushing upward thousands of feet like huge mounds of leavened dough. It was happening. Some threshold had been breached. The sky darkened like a hematoma and the desert grew still as a black phalanx approached from the south dragging curtains of virga. Then there was a low drum of thunder. And another, its rhythm gathering momentum. As the wind rose on the storm's pressure wave I could smell the rain. A desert scent of wet dust stained with creosote. The first fat, cold drops turned me back down the trail. The thunder sent me running. Flashes of lightning and great detonations drove me on, stumbling, mindless, my heart pounding. The trail was too steep and too slick; my feet kept slipping out of my wet sandals. I wanted to pull them off and continue barefoot, but I was afraid to stop. I felt like a target, exposed on the hillside where the air smelled like ozone and whined with electricity.

By the time I reached home, soaked and shivering, the storm had passed. Wrapped in a towel at my window, I watched gloaming come to the mountains in a frenetic display of shadow and sun-shaft.

That night, Karen's water broke. Without waking me, she showered and gathered a few things, preparing for the two-hour ride to the hospital. At six in the morning she packed me into the truck. I told her I couldn't go. I needed to ring the wake-up bell in an hour, and it was my turn to lead flag-raising and chapel services.

At the Circle K in Oracle, I stopped for gas. I had messed up. I was supposed to keep the tank full; Karen had left this up to me as my only pre-labor responsibility. Now we were in a hurry, so I asked Karen if she wouldn't mind paying the cashier while I pumped the gas. She sat in her seat, looking at me with disbelief.

Halfway to the hospital she wanted a bathroom. We were in the middle of some cotton fields on the Gila River Indian Reservation, and I hadn't seen anyone else on the road, so I pulled over near an irrigation canal. She got out. I stood guard. Karen could handle anything, I thought at the time. She could have filled the tank and driven herself to the hospital. What did she need me for? Perhaps her confidence made me feel inadequate; maybe that's why I behaved like I didn't care about her anymore. She missed the way I used to pursue her when we were courting, how I watched her from across the room whenever she walked in, and how I planned secret meetings with her on some hilltop. Now, married, it was as if I had won a prize and displayed it on a shelf. The intense, pro-longed energy of courtship had waned into irregular bursts of static whenever we made love. We might as well have been rubbing our feet across a carpet. I should have known that Karen just needed simple things. Mostly my attention. Instead of watching for cars on that road-side, she needed me to hold her hand while she peed.

The hospital admitted her immediately. Karen's labor pains had grown strong, her contractions only minutes apart as the nurses prepped her, and I fumbled with booties, mask, and gown. The baby was coming. Karen insisted on a natural birth; she wanted full control. No stirrups. No needles. No drugs. As the nurses entered and left the room, I overheard them several times refer to her as "the one without the IVs." My primary delivery room job was to see that they honored her requests.

When the baby's head came the doctor called it a "textbook" crown. Look at this, he said to the nurses. One of them wheeled in a mirror so Karen could see. Karen made an attempt at getting up, then raised her voice: Okay! Let's get on with it. When the doctor asked her to push I thought she looked strange. Her eyes were wide and her cheeks puffed and red. Something was different from the practice sessions. I asked her what she was doing. I'm having a baby, what are you doing? she said before the next contraction came.

At eight-twenty, Jessica slipped into the cold and glare of the hospital room. Immediately, she began to cry. Her wet skin looked purple, but as her tiny puckered face began to squall, she flushed to pink. I held her like my first kitten at age six. A girl! I told Karen without looking at her. We have a girl!

I spent that day and the next waterskiing with Tom and some of the staff from camp. It was a day off I had been planning on for weeks. Karen spent the time arguing with the nurses and doctors about her release, finally convincing them to let her sign the forms and take her baby home. When I picked her up at the hospital the next evening, thirty-six hours after

Jessica's birth, she was quiet, upset. Later she told me that the nurses kept asking where I was, and she had felt disappointed that I hadn't been there to support her decision for early checkout, disappointed and ashamed.

Darkness had settled over the hills when the three of us arrived at camp. Pulling up to our residence, I could smell the rain. Our feet crunched on wet ground, and lightning played with the night sky on the northern horizon. The porch light glowed, and like a neon sign above a singles bar, it invited winged creatures to socialize and find mates. I admired those monsoon-aroused insects. The males especially had it made. Their only paternal investment involved supplying seed. After a night's nuptial frenzy, they would die, leaving their mates to raise their progeny. To me, this task—putting up with the opposite sex solely for the purpose of reproduction—so suited females; it was nature's conditioning from birth.

Within a week, Karen was back inside her tight, white jeans, much to the chagrin of the women on the staff. A source of pride for her. But, although she had dropped from 130 to 112, she was obviously a new mother—and not only because she *couldn't* fit into her pre-pregnancy blouses. She had changed. She had a new priority, a new focus in her life. I, on the other hand, had just begun to deal with the idea of being a father.

I write this now, just after Jessica's eleventh birthday, knowing that I never did figure it out. I wish I could say that things got better, that I got better. That Karen, instead of putting up with me and patiently waiting through my faults, finally saw me adjust to being a parent, a husband. But, tragically—despicably on my part—during Karen's third pregnancy, three years after Jessica was born, I was on my way to prison. In the midst of my struggle to accept and understand fatherhood, I had abandoned it all—my marriage and family, my teaching career. I've left Karen to raise our children on her own, while I've sat in prison for eight years convincing myself I could do better with a second chance. The irony is that our girls will be grown before I'm released. And Karen is a different woman.

Second chances are meaningless; there is no going back. Some things can't be forgiven. But forgiveness isn't really important. Or necessary.

What matters now is that Karen believes I'm worth salvaging. Under the signature scars of my past mistakes, she's noticed something I'm only beginning to recognize—something brooding, awakening in me. Clarity and vision born of a flawed character? The wisdom of regret? Possibly. One thing's certain, though. I'm not starting over. Karen hasn't given me a second chance or a new beginning. She's given me something greater. Like those summer monsoons in the desert, she's given me the promise of continuing.

beneath the scroll

We parked the car at a cattle guard and unloaded packs, canteens, flashlights, and climbing gear. After scaling a barbed-wire fence, we crossed a cattle-razed field studded with warty conglomerate rocks and prickly pear cactus among a few dead hummocks of grass. Dried cow pats marked a path that disappeared where we descended into a wide valley. Somewhere on that slope was the entrance to the cave, but we'd missed it. It happened every time. Unaided by trails or signs, we usually walked right past the opening without noticing it. So much the better; fewer people to mess things up. Separated and zigzagging, we checked every limestone outcrop for a black wound that split open the hillside and dropped hundreds of feet into the earth.

We'd come to the northern slopes of the Santa Catalina Mountains, north of Tucson, Arizona, to explore a limestone solution cavern known as Scroll Cave. Nothing official. Two friends, Jeff Teich and Terry Hutch-

---

Above: Figure-eight with locking carabiner

/ 33 /

ins, had met my wife and me earlier that morning in Peppersauce Canyon, where we had been camping. They had plans to spend a fall weekend spelunking and wanted me to come along with them. Karen stayed in camp with our daughters, two-and-a-half-year-old Jessica and eleven-month-old Kasondra, finding her excitement in the safe pages of a book (although she said the real reason for remaining behind was to be available for a necessary rescue). I decided to join the two adventurers for a subterranean excursion.

Terry, Jeff, and I had been friends since we met at the YMCA camp in 1980, the summer following the one when Karen and I fell in love. Terry, an experienced rock climber and the instigator of that day's trip, was the bedrock of our group. His lucid thinking, requisite for teaching junior high science, I suppose, generally kept us out of trouble. Jeff, a college business professor, was more open-minded, approachable, and eager to try new things, especially if they shocked people. He had recently developed a fondness for nude sunbathing while visiting the beaches of Greece, a fondness he carried back with him to the states—much to my wife's discomfort whenever he casually dropped his shorts. Jeff, like me, enjoyed taking chances, although I generally kept my clothes on.

I was breathing hard when we found the cave. The search had warmed me and loosened muscles stiff from the rough ride up the mountain. I dropped a coil of skyline rope and stripped off my Levi's jacket. Once inside, I wouldn't need the extra clothing; even my sweatshirt would be too much in the cave's unchanging seventy-two-degree environment. Terry drove a piton into a boulder above the cave, hooked on a carabiner, and secured the skyline. Jeff and I slipped on diaper harnesses. We decided to make our descent in two parts: a forty-foot rappel to a wide ledge followed by a thirty-foot ropeless scramble through a tight chute. Although we could have crawled in another way without climbing gear, we enjoyed the more direct approach.

My friends elected me to initiate our coital descent into Scroll Cave. Terry pushed a loop of rope through a figure-eight and handed it to me. I clipped it into the locking carabiner at my waist and tightened the screw.

The aluminum was cold. My fingers grew numb and as pale as slugs as I gripped the rope and backed away from the security of firm footing. I'd done this dozens of times before, but the transition from trusting my legs to trusting the rope always unnerved me. There's an awkward, groin-quivering instant when you lose control before you feel the rope's support. Light faded as I stepped down vertical walls to the dusty ledge.

Terry and Jeff followed, one after another, slipping out of a broad crack of light like frightened spiders. We gave our eyes time to adjust, unpacking helmets and flashlights and leaving the ropes and harnesses. Below, a narrow rift sloped away from us at a steep angle. We wedged our bodies between its surfaces and continued our descent, chimneying with flashlights in our mouths. It was at this point, halfway down, when my arms and legs began to tremble, that I always had the same vision: a marble ricocheting through a rain gutter. But then I heard myself say: *Adventure means risk.* It's not adventure unless it threatens you somehow, promises to bloody your knuckles, break your legs, give you a concussion. Death by exposure. Dehydration, starvation, hypothermia. It's not true adventure unless it can kill you.

With spelunking, a quick death would be merciful. A broken leg might mean an agonizing end if you're lost and alone like waking up in a leaking coffin after being buried alive: no amount of screaming or pounding will make any difference. But who wants adventure with safety nets? You might as well watch television or read books. Adventure is like romance; there must be some lack of confidence, moments of uncertainty, distrust, restrictions on time, limitations of ability, even discomfort, pain. These add challenge, heighten the experience. While I was courting my wife, focusing all my attention on her, these romantic elements made simply being together thrilling. Our relationship was all question marks: Did she look in my direction? Is she interested in me? Will she meet me alone tonight? And again tomorrow? I never knew what to expect with her; every step was terra incognita. One slip could have finished us. Once we were married and grew more familiar with each other, I wondered if the adventure was over. What excitement can there be on solid ground? In an institution? (Why do people call both marriage and prison an institution? And why are both something you must be committed to?) If I wanted romance, I had to go spelunking.

Karen, I'm afraid, would never understand this wanderlust of mine. She accepted it as another testosterone impairment, a fact of nature in conflict with her nesting instinct, the yin and yang of the marriage bond. Men are forever exploring, hunting, and, she hoped, providing. (Do we work to fill the larder or work for self-fulfillment?) Karen just wanted security. Her adventure, undoubtedly, arose from creating clever ways to pull me along in the direction of her innate need to pour all resources into raising a family. If I required romance, then she would offer it by reminding me that she was still terra incognita: *What makes you think,* I can hear her say, even after thirteen years of marriage, *that one slip even now won't finish you?*

Her humor occasionally had a sharp point to it. That day she joked about standing by for our rescue, and I think she was halfway serious. She'd bailed me out of other blunders, cleaning up after me, bandaging wounds, plugging holes where my brain had leaked. And she would again. Perhaps the reason she joined me so often was to keep me out of trouble. Even if I never thought about it, she must have considered what consequences would fall to her if I left on some excursion and never returned, left her alone to care for our children. Thinking about this now makes me feel ashamed—the risks I've taken to satisfy myself, the stupid mistakes. Is taking risks part of my nature or something I've learned? Am I testosterone impaired . . . or character flawed?

The air lay humid and warm against my skin and smelled like ripe garden compost. After we dropped into the first cavern, I felt the dead weight of enclosure, but my flashlight revealed a large circular room. The ceiling twisted into hidden recesses, chambers, and intersecting crevices beyond my light's detection. Broken shards of rock littered the uneven floor, making my footing unsure, dangerous. The bladed edges of the largest rocks waited in the dark to assault my shins. We picked through the loose scree and followed a decline to another passage leading deeper into the mountain. Limestone formations appeared. Like frozen roots, soda straw stalactites hovered breathlessly above our heads. Within jagged cuts and joints, delicate helicites seemed to defy gravity, poised like hundreds of bent, misdriven nails. In the next room, huge stalactites hung above rising stalagmite mounds, some joining in great marble columns to cast shadows of obsessive geometry. Fountains of milky flowstone poured from high vaulted lofts, rippling and cascading to the floor in solidified abandon. Earth tones prevailed: cream and amber to rose and umber, a spectrum borrowed from compositions of minerals and dust.

I sat in the mud next to an undulating staircase of flowstone. Its surface felt clammy and moist. Wetness was good; it meant that the cave was alive and growing. Droplets of water leaking from the ceiling, trickling down walls, and splattering on the floor eventually deposit enough minerals to create wonderful natural sculptures, given the time. A thousand years may pass before one cubic inch of stalactite accumulates.

Pristine, suggestive shapes in caves may have an erotic quality—due, it seems, to the inescapable metaphor of the act of spelunking itself. It's part of the aesthetics, I guess. But it was the purity of these formations that attracted me, an immaculacy born of inaccessibility. Few people clamber around in caves by rope and lamp. Most want guided tours, phones, aide stations, and other conveniences. *Wouldn't a restaurant here be nice, perhaps near the elevator?* They are the culture Edward Abbey confronted in the canyonlands of Utah. Windshield tourists who never get out of their cars. Fine. Some places shouldn't have lighted paths. We could do away with a few roads, too. Preserving inaccessibility is what makes adventurers like spelunkers secretive; they are a quiet, even elite club. They protect this inaccessibility by keeping the locations of their passion hidden from those outside. Or they bar the entrances with heavy steel doors and locks and keys. In this, they hope to keep caves like Scroll wild, unblemished.

I am a fanatic of cloistered places; I've seen what uncontrolled access does. Not far from Scroll, thoughtless people descended upon another cave after a newspaper gave away its location. Peppersauce Cave, once remarkable in its crawlways, clear pools, and limestone formations, is now no more than a mud hole. Only a hundred yards from a road, it's become a popular place for weekend partiers to violate. Broken bottles, beer cans, batteries, string, empty potato chip bags and other trash clutter its rooms; spray paint, giving directions in a cave that has only one entrance and exit, mars its walls. The formations are gone, broken stubs of calcite only hint at their former magnificence. My daughters will only be able to imagine the Peppersauce Cave I once knew. I'll always believe in limited access. Even if it means I'm the one who's limited.

In a corner of the grotto where I sat, Jeff found a passageway filled with rocky debris. He was attracted to a fresh current of air emerging from the seemingly insignificant hole. The portal, concealed by spelunkers who wanted its reaches left undiscovered, at least to the novice caver, was little more than the diameter of Jeff's shoulders. Jeff wanted to explore it, but I'd crawled through its intricate system of claustrophobic worm holes before. I'd survived the Torture Chamber and kneeled beneath the Scroll, a stalactite that unfurls from the ceiling like a roll of upended parchment. The memory of getting there made me shiver. For hundreds of yards I had inched along the tubes with my arms out front, pushing with my toes, the weight of tons of rock pressing on my sanity. I could not back out. If I pulled my arms to my sides I risked getting stuck—not a pleasant predicament. I had to continue, hoping to find enough room to turn around. Finding a dead end would have been just that, a dead end. It was exhausting, knee- and elbow-abrading work. The humidity, my sweat, and the mud made a wretched composition on my skin and clothes, staining both with iron oxide clay. One trip satisfied my curiosity, but I knew, because curiosity is never really satisfied, I'd do it again. I had to. Just not this time.

Terry suggested that the three of us explore another area in the opposite direction. I agreed, and Jeff reluctantly followed us. The curve of the rock in the penumbra of our lights was pitted and gnarled with great convolutions like obese, wrinkled folds of tissue. Something heavy in the air clung to the lining of my lungs. The dampness played with sound. Our footfalls echoed from the walls and droned around our ears.

We scrambled over a raised deck along a dilating corridor that curled to the right and emptied into a vestibule. In the lower corner of the solution chamber, a passage opened into a small alcove. A lobe of flowstone dominated the center, drooping halfway to the floor. The room seemed an appropriate place to spend a few moments before returning to the surface. One after another we climbed inside, took a seat around the flowstone, and turned off our lights.

Darkness and silence enveloped us. The blackness was absolute, tangible. There, darkness was a physical thing. I felt its sweaty embrace, its heavy breath, but at the same time I sensed no benevolence. The darkness poked at me where I was vulnerable. My mind couldn't erase the fact that I was far underground, nearly buried except for an unspooled thread of an airway leading to the outside world. If, on a whim, the mountain shuddered, I would have become a fossil, curled in fetal position between limestone plates. I reached a hand into the blackness and only found an ambiance of rock. I found no security in my touching. This is adventure, I told myself, realizing then that I might not believe it until later. Afterwards, I would remember the fear and insecurity and danger within another context, one where I had control, where I could look back and laugh.

When I'd had enough, I checked my flashlight to see that it still worked. Terry and Jeff did likewise. When we spoke, the room answered back in low tones. Fascinated, we experimented with a few deep notes until we had the right key. Instantly, the whole chamber responded, amplifying and carrying our resonant chant as if we were Trappist monks in the Abbey of Gethsemane. We were making music with the mountain in visceral harmony, music that seemed to come from nowhere yet everywhere, filling the chamber with the body of its sound. "Wild surroundings often set me humming," Scott Russell Sanders says after describing how matching vocal pitch with a New England stream made him feel connected to the water flowing around him. It was the same there, with that buried stone. It was as if we were part of the mountain's own throat.

Back at our campsite, trees and canyon walls stretched shadows as the sun prepared to join the western ridges. The world below had seemed timeless, unmarked by the changing days or seasons as our familiar solar calendar measures them. Scroll Cave records time as minute degrees of physical change on a vast geologic scale. Having enjoyed a few weak experiences there, I could say that and still not fully comprehend it. One thing I did understand: my tenure on earth is short, and I cannot fool myself into believing that there is enough time to do anything significant, lasting. Was I substituting that kind of escapism for what was really significant: my place as a husband and father, my place as a teacher? Probably. I had hardly even thought about my family while underground. I only knew that I had to hunt for adventure, hunt for it because it wouldn't find me, and for me, finding it was the difference between living and being.

That day, I gratified myself with a few scraps, a taste—the feel of cold limestone against my skin, earth untouched by sunlight, the wet breath of a dark and living place. It wouldn't be enough; it never had been. Adventure, also like romance, is addictive. It's never enough, except for right now.

Linda Hogan says that caves are not the places for men. "They are a feminine world, a womb of earth, a germinal place of brooding." I know this is true, at least with me. I enter caves only for pleasure, for the challenge. I take and give nothing back. Realizing this now, I should never return to Scroll, and I shouldn't write about it or tell anyone of its location. I shouldn't, because there are other exciting inner journeys that are more important. Marriage is one. Spending the day with our daughters at our campsite, Karen had it right all along: motherhood is real adventure. Raising children well is risk enough, as the only truly meaningful, even eternal thing we can do.

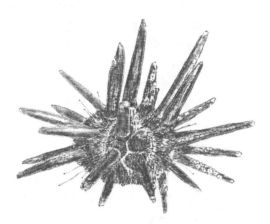

oceanic rifts

By my last year of teaching in public school in 1986, my classroom had
spilled over into an after-school taxidermy workshop, an annual cooking
and eating event we called "the Beast Feast," and a science club, which
traveled around the state on monthly wilderness expeditions. My
wildlife collections, caged and displayed in the classroom, attracted students I never taught in class. I built terrariums for protected toads and rattlesnakes and ringtails. I hatched quail in a homemade incubator and
occasionally brought in Harris' hawks I had trained in falconry. I set up
freshwater aquariums for fish taken from local streams, and coral reef
tanks for marine invertebrates smuggled into Arizona from the ocean.
My classroom, like my childhood bedroom, was a hissing, squawking,
bubbling menagerie, and I enjoyed being its central attraction.

Early that same year, our science club traveled to Mexico to experience
a place where, less than sixty-five miles south of the border, the Sonoran

---

Above: Pencil urchin *(Eucidaris thouarsii)*

Desert meets the Gulf of California. I had often visited "Arizona's Coast" while a student at the University of Arizona, and although the quiet beaches offered a favorite respite for students on spring break, I had another reason for venturing there—a fascination with tide pools and mud flats. So, while other college kids packed volleyballs, swimsuits, and suntan lotion, I packed dip nets, flashlights, field guides, and portable fish tanks (which allowed me to extract a bit of ocean for my desert home). On later trips, I infected my wife and friends with my attraction to the place, but that January of 1986 was the first time I would be responsible for a dozen children in a foreign country.

Near the end of Mexican Highway 8, the first thing you notice is the smell: a warm and wet pungency that leaves a wonderful residue on your palate like sun-dried brine shrimp. In the distance the sky pales and shimmers in the sun. A fine white sand, driven into billows by wind, hems the road. The dunes, ragged with gray vegetation, emerge from a range of gnat-black mountains and dive toward the horizon where the whole desiccated landscape suddenly plunges beneath a brilliant blue expanse. Here, even the desert succumbs to the allure of the sea.

Although we wouldn't explore those volcanic mountains that time, their jagged skyline recalled for me other excursions there and reminded me of this desert's desperate barrenness. Only a few roads broke away from the asphalt and meandered westward where drifting sand either swallowed them or ancient lava flows barricaded them altogether. Withered brittlebushes complained of thirst by rasping against the undercarriage of your vehicle. Traveling there was uncertain; wandering lost many miles from civilization, likely.

On the peninsula of Sinai about thirty-five hundred years ago, Moses struck the rock and water gushed into the wilderness. Some four to six million years ago, a globe-circling system of oceanic ridges called the East Pacific Rise struck what is now western Mexico and an ocean spilled into another wilderness. The rift unzipped the Baja peninsula from the mainland, shearing the landscape northwestward through California's Salton Trough, where it now becomes indistinguishable from the San Andreas

Fault. Magma, welling up into the seam, continues to dilate the ocean floor and widen the Gulf, as the North Pacific basin rotates counter-clockwise, wrenching Baja and southern California away from the rest of North America.

The resulting volcanism at the head of the Gulf of California has created one of the most inhospitable places in the world. The late Edward Abbey called it "the bleakest, flattest, hottest, grittiest, grimmest, dreariest, ugliest, most useless, most senseless desert of them all." John Van Dyke, at the turn of last century, described it this way: "Volcanoes have left their traces everywhere. You can still see the streams of lava that have chilled as they ran . . . there are great lakes and streams of reddish-black lava, frozen in swirls and pools, cracked like glass, broken into blocks like a ruined pavement."

This is the Pinacate Desert, a 750-square-mile wasteland named for a diminutive black beetle—the pinacate beetle—most commonly called a stink bug. It is the region's mascot. At the center of this place of cinder cones, craters, fumaroles, collapsed calderas, and lava fields, dome-shaped Pinacate Peak rises 3,957 feet above sea level. To the south and west of the volcano, salt marshes and sand dunes border the Gulf of California. On the north and east, low granite mountains, smudged with cacti and creosote, poke up through the desert floor. Only a prophet, or a solitary stink bug, it seems, would choose to live here.

One of the first scientists to describe the region, more than two centuries after Father Eusebio Francisco Kino ventured here in 1689, was zoologist William T. Hornaday, who came to the Pinacate Desert with an expedition in the fall of 1907. At the time he was director of the New York Zoological Park, previously having been chief taxidermist with the U.S. National Museum. Two members of his team, Daniel T. MacDougal, the botanist who convinced Hornaday to make the trip, and Godfrey Sykes, both worked for the newly established Carnegie Desert Botanical Laboratory in Tucson, Arizona. MacDougal was its director.

After leaving Tucson, the expedition traveled west through Papagueria (the reservation of today's Tohono O'odham) to the tiny Mexican village of Sonoyta. From the spring at Quitobaquito, a "lonesome, stagnant, out-of-the-way-place," as Hornaday described its inches-wide stream and small pond, the group took a circuitous route into the Pinacate Desert, first following the Sonoyta River south, then heading northward into the infamous bone yard of El Camino del Diablo, the "Devil's Highway." Finally entering the lava field itself from the northwest, they located and named two volcanic craters before camping at Papago Tanks. Hornaday hunted bighorn sheep and pronghorn, taking spirited side trips to collect the largest specimens, but all along he seemed most impressed with the plants that survived on the stark lava. He carved open the occasional small barrel cacti he called "bisnagas" and chewed their pulp to determine their moisture quality. He noted twisted elephant trees or "torote," ironwood and smoke trees, tree cholla, and saguaros that "on account of the scarcity of water and total lack of soil, the straggling specimens of it were very small and limbless."

On November 20, 1907, after traveling farther south to camp at Tule Tank, the expedition at last climbed Pinacate Peak. From its summit Hornaday wrote: "This huge basin between the three peaks once was the crater of this culminating volcano; and the peaks themselves when united formed the rim. First a notch was blown out toward the west, through which we came. Later on another one, much deeper, was blown out toward the south. Through these two notches ran great rivers of molten lava, and the congealed mass is there today, almost the same as when it came hot from the kettles of Pluto. . . ."

In most of the Pinacate Desert, where sunlight strips the landscape clean of even shadow, life is minimized. Only at the margins, where sand wrestles with lava and shrubs like brittlebush find advantage, might you find a few rock-dark lizards chasing beetles and scorpions, marking their comings and goings with water-stingy, pastelike droppings. Brittlebush, a conspicuous low shrub that looks more dead than alive, favors the outwash slopes of the volcanic hills and the lava-sand boundaries where runoff occasionally collects. Its variable leaves become large and fleshy after the occasional winter and summer rains, then small and furry during the drought. The bone-white plant also leaches a toxin into the soil that prevents other plants from germinating close by, where they might preempt essential resources like water.

A few thin saguaro cacti, most obstinate in this place, lean into the broken slopes of the mountains. Where the basalt rock has crumbled, teddy bear cholla also gain a foothold. Where the sand has reclaimed a slip of lava, caucuses of spindly mesquite trees rest in a kind of fugue state among locoweed and sand verbena, waiting mostly in vain for rain. Other sources of water are only semipermanent, stagnating in two or three widely dispersed catchment basins called *tinajas*, "earthen jars." In this desert, where plants and animals are narrowed down into seams, life must make atonement for itself.

The first time I strayed into the Pinacate, my road followed the contours of a lava flow to a place where the black wall eventually allowed me access to its surface above the sand. A broad, flat pavement, like hardened resin, spread out before me. From the elevated bench I could make out the dimensions of the flow. Its source spilled from one side of Pinacate Peak to the north as a tarlike discharge. From there, the lava slipped toward the sea, with dark fingers escaping the main body and pointing out alternate routes over an uneven terrain covering many square miles. The effect was dramatic, dead serious. I stopped the truck and stepped out onto the crust of Venus stripped of its atmospheric pressure and heat. Silence laid its hand on me. Nothing moved. The air offered no breeze in way of apology. A rock I tossed a few feet in front of me rang in my ears with a sound like breaking porcelain. I stood on an altar of basalt in the sun, but I wasn't prepared to make any sacrifices, then or now.

Near midnight, we had bypassed the worst of the Pinacate Desert to arrive at a tiny peninsula called Pelican Point on the Gulf of California— two trucks, a van, five adults, and a dozen children. The youngest were Karen's and mine: Jessica, nearly three, and her one-year-old sister Kasondra. Great shadowed dunes, double-stitched together by the tracks of foraging beetles, backed up our campsite on the beach. A bloated fish-belly moon crossed a clear sky, promising exceptionally low tides.

From our campsite, the coastline arced wide to the south where the lights of the small fishing town of Puerto Peñasco wavered like new constellations low in the sky. To the north, the beach rose into the black rocks of Pelican Point. From there, I knew from previous visits, the coastline retreated somewhere behind us, fronting the gringo shantytown of Cholla Bay before circling away and sinking beneath a salt marsh.

Cholla Bay itself, the southernmost pocket of Bahia Adair, named for the cholla cactus forest just beyond the marsh, is one of those wonderful places where low tides reveal vast tracts of shallow sea floor. Spring tides, which happen twice a month during the full and new moon, occur due to the combined gravitational influences of the sun and moon. In conjunction with the bay's topography, they produce the greatest high and low tides, uncovering places normally inundated and providing opportunities for observing arrays of creatures inhabiting underwater plains of mud and silt. By morning, I knew, the earth would again rotate from beneath the current tidal bulge and the whole bay would empty, exposing many miles of walkable mud flats shimmering with shallow, silted rivulets, eddies, and pools.

While Karen arranged the back of our camper-shelled truck for sleeping, I led a group of students down to the water's edge for the ritual greeting—a face-wetting, briny kiss to insure perfect weather. After driving through the desert for hours I felt ecstatic, emotionally high on the salt air and the promise of adventure and exploration in a place I loved. Sharing this place with students whom I enjoyed teaching made my mind race with ideas and expectations. Sleep was impossible. Instead, I went for a run along the glimmering beach.

When I returned, Karen was already asleep in the truck with our daughters curled next to her. The van, where the parents of one of my students had arranged their own beds, was quiet. The boys and girls had divided up into two groups, laying out tarps and sleeping bags on the sand above the tide line. Terry Hutchins, the real force behind our science club, had dragged his bag to a strategic place between them and lay motionless. I dropped onto the boy's tarp.

"Where are you going to sleep?" one of the girls asked from across the sand, probably hoping that I would join my family in the truck and not spoil their plans for unsupervised fun.

"I don't know, Erica," I answered, recognizing her high, impudent voice. "Maybe right here."

She couldn't conceal her disappointment.

It was then that I called the whole group together to express my expectations, surprising my students with my own plans. I didn't want to be their "teacher"; I wanted to relate to them as I did with the children at the YMCA camp, where an authoritarian presence was generally unneeded and thus less severe, where the gulf between youth and adult was still narrow and navigable. I asked them to think of me as a counselor and as a friend, and I asked them to call me by my first name.

"Can we stay up all night, *Ken?*" Luke asked, testing our new relationship. Unlike his quiet best friend, Brian, Luke was always the first to test the boundaries and sometimes to cross them.

"I don't know about you," I said, "but I won't be able to sleep."

I learned the next day that Terry had overheard our conversation and at the time thought my answer was a brilliant use of reverse psychology; he never imagined I could be serious. The events that followed that night, I believe now, began a widening that was eventually to split apart our friendship, as it would all my relationships.

We didn't sleep that night. Instead, we passed the early morning hours roaming the sand dunes, playing games we invented like "Pumice Wars," which involved throwing the light, soft volcanic rocks at each other, and a team version of hide-and-seek we called "Ditch 'em." When the tide began to recede, giant, shining-black rocks rose up along the shoreline like a herd of dark cattle moving in to graze on new pasture. Six of us followed the tide out and quietly climbed onto one of the largest rocks, wrapping ourselves in blankets and facing the flat water to wait for sunrise.

"What are those lights?" Brian asked after a long silence.

"Shrimp boats," I answered. "They'll be coming in with the next high tide. We should go into town later today and buy some fresh shrimp to add to the crabs and clams we'll collect for tonight's dinner."

Loud screams and laughing from the beach periodically interrupted our reverie. I had just begun considering expending the energy to quiet them before they woke the adults in the vehicles when Luke asked, "Is that Mr. Hutchins?"

Behind us, a dark shape was stumbling our way among the boulders. "I think so," someone offered. "But what's he wearing?"

Terry, limping barefoot across the barnacle-studded rocks, had wrapped himself in his sleeping bag before coming to find me. "Do you know what time it is?" he yelled at me. "It's after four in the morning! I'm sure these kids' parents would be happy about knowing what they're doing out this late. If you won't make them go to bed then I will!" And then he turned around and hobbled back up the beach.

I never said a word.

Dew coated everything by morning. I struggled to work off the chill by unpacking gear, while Karen fixed breakfast and Terry handed out dip nets and buckets to the students with free hands who hadn't adopted Jessica and Kasondra. We had decided to spend the morning low tide at Pelican Point and then drive over to Cholla Bay for the evening ebb tide. The water had retreated hundreds of feet, revealing boulders out on the flat limestone shelves called coquina. Low tide at Pelican Point gave us an entirely different kind of exploration—tide-pooling. Tide pools form in rocky basins and catchments as the tide recedes, placing invertebrates and fishes within easy access of curious faces. They are microhabitats, disrupted and remade twice a day with every tide cycle. In them, various phyla of animals—sponges, coelenterates, worms, mollusks, arthropods, echinoderms, and chordates—sputter and froth to survive the changes. A single tide pool, like a classroom aquarium, offers a wondrous miniature world to the casual observer. No special tools or knowledge are necessary.

In her book about the Cape Region of Baja California, Ann Zwinger describes tide pools as "so still, in muted rose, coral, and olive, neutral tans and beiges. No bright colors at all. Tiny waterfalls between pools adjust the levels until there is no more adjustment to be done. The sound of the ocean diminishes and the landward sounds emerge, quiet poppings and clickings, tiny smackings as drying begins." On the northeast coast of the same gulf and a hundred yards from shore, my students and I crouched in awe on the rim of a similar world less than two feet deep. The water held perfectly still and clear, and sunlight illuminated the whole pool as though the rock and sand and water were glowing themselves.

Movement was everywhere. The slender arms of brittle stars poked out along the perimeter of the pool, sweeping, groping, entwining, the animals' vulnerable disks secured in the crevices. Brick-red pencil urchins also held tight against our inquisitive fingers, using their stubby spines to wedge themselves between the rocks. Scores of hermit crabs scuttled over one another, their shells the dispossessed homes of snails. Shoals of fishes, bottom-dwelling speckled blennies and striped sergeant majors, patrolled every liquid recess searching for food.

I turned over a rock and uncovered a hidden zoo. A chorus of *Ooh*'s escaped us as a thumb-sized octopus jetted away, leaving a black button of ink hanging in its place. The remains of its meal, a half-empty carapace of a crab, settled on the sand, legs pointing to the sky. Variegated brittle stars, suddenly in the open, scrambled for cover in three different directions. A "fire worm," a segmented ribbon armed with a coat of poisonous glass spicules, double-coiled and then retreated again under the rock. Sedentary creatures encrusted the rock's exposed underside. Patches of orange and yellow sponges looked like spilled paint. Eight-plated chitons, primitive relatives of snails, defied my students' most dexterous attempts to pry them loose. One member of a congregation of dark green sea cucumbers squirted a fine stream of seawater that rippled the surface of the pool. I replaced the rock while a pavement of colonial anemones watched us with a hundred, bulging, half-closed eyes.

By late morning the sun reflected hard against the dark blue of high tide, scattering fish scales of light along the crests and troughs of tiny swells. Farther out, bottom vegetation mottled the water with deep azure and deeper cerulean, beneath a horizon flat and empty to the edge of sight. A rising breeze carried south and seaward along the coastline.

While many of the students braved the sixty-degree water for a swim, I inflated a one-man yellow boat of the same drugstore, rubber-ducky, river-runner kind made popular by Ed Abbey. Since high tide meant feeding fish, I planned on floating in it to drag a baited hook across the rocky bottom and catch a few shrimp-tasty triggerfish for dinner.

"Can we use your boat?" Erica asked seconds after I had finished blowing it up.

"A minute ago you were laughing at me. Now you want me to do you a favor?"

"We won't be gone too long," her friend added.

Fifteen minutes later, I noticed Karen looking down the beach. "Ken," she said. "Are those girls in your boat?"

I looked in the direction she was staring and saw a tiny yellow speck on the water. The two girls, their paddles waving like pelican wings, had allowed the wind to push them far down the beach and away from shore. With Brian, Luke, and other students following me, I ran along the wet margin of sand and then crossed out onto a spit of coquina until I was within shouting distance.

"What are you doing?" I yelled at them. "Paddle that thing back here!"

"We can't!" one of them answered. "We don't know how!"

The girls could only send the boat in circles. "Try working together," I suggested, "in the same direction, toward the beach." When I realized my instructions were hopeless, and that the boat continued to drift farther out to sea, I dove into the water and swam to them. They were unappreciative. "Move over," I said, throwing my upper body into the boat and kicking toward shore.

"We were doing fine," Erica insisted. "You didn't have to be a hero and rescue us. Now everyone is watching."

This was true. The locals, a few tourists, and most of our group were now looking in our direction. "I don't care," I said. Then they began complaining that I was getting water in the boat. "How come you're both so dry?" I asked, my feet finding the sandy bottom. The look on their faces told me they knew what was coming. I slipped off the boat and lifted it out of the water, spilling the girls into the sea. Dragging the boat to the beach, I heard Erica yelling something about her shoes as her friend, her blond hair flat against her face, launched herself at me and knocked me into the water. Now the boys came to my aid, splashing foam and sand and laughing at the girls' screams. All the way back to our campsite, we chased each other in and out of the waves, throwing handfuls of sand and wet strings of seaweed into each other's hair.

In the evening, as Cholla Bay emptied its brackish contents, we climbed down the stairway behind JJ's Cantina and stepped onto the mud flats. Although we walked carefully, we still unavoidably crunched over carpets of mud snails feeding on black detritus. It smelled of raw sewage. Beyond the mud snails, we found sweet potato-like sea hares; deadly, fish-eating cone shells; and a fist-sized pink *Murex*. Farther out, as darkness came, our flashlights illuminated beds of half-buried, scavenging sand dollars—not the white skeletons of beach-combers, but bristling, wine-colored, living disks. In protest to being disturbed, an arrowhead-shaped sand dollar stained my hands Tyrian purple. About a mile from the shoreline, the backwater was knee deep. Two swimming crabs threatened us when we cut off their escape, snapping at the surface with giant blue claws. I scooped them up in my net and dumped them into a bucket of clams Karen had been collecting.

In the deep water we located tube anemones, christened "sloppy guts" by Tiny Colleto, a Mexican seaman and crew member of the 1940 Ricketts and Steinbeck expedition to the Gulf, because the "encased body is very ugly, like rotting gray cloth." The silt and mucus tubes of these animals may extend three feet into the mud. Their delicate magenta and purple tentacles created an exquisite bouquet against a carbon background. Resembling thread-petalled flowers, the anemones use tentacles lined with stinging cells to capture tiny crustaceans and fish. When a small animal touches a tentacle, the stinging cells discharge, gripping and paralyzing it. The anemone then draws its victim into its mouth.

Like waterlogged Nerf balls, bright orange tunicates floated by us, warning us of the returning tide. Karen lifted a scarlet gorgonian coral drifting in the water and shined her light through it. It looked like a strange Oriental fan but was actually a colony of animals related to sea anemones, each slender branchlet home to thousands of individual polyps armed with tiny tentacles for feeding on the bay's rich plankton. Both the coral and the tunicates had broken away from a nearby sponge reef, but the tide wouldn't allow us time to find it and remain dry.

With our daughters asleep in our arms, Karen and I followed the string of the students' flashlights back to JJ's and our parked vehicles. Our feet were raw and sore from walking in wet, sand-ridden tennis shoes, but Karen didn't complain. She had other concerns on her mind. Terry hadn't spoken to me all day, and she had noticed.

"He's still upset about last night," she said.

"I know. He's been nervous this whole trip, and I'm not helping him much."

"He really cares about you, you know. He doesn't want to see something stupid happen." Terry wasn't the only one who had become concerned about my behavior. Karen, too, was worried. Lately, she had begun siding with parents and teachers against me, an unusual position for her.

When I finally talked to Terry, he wanted everyone in their sleeping bags by ten. "I'll tell them if you don't want to," he said to me. I told him that I would take care of it, which I did, blaming the reason for the early curfew on my friend.

We prepared a late dinner on the beach, frying breaded triggerfish in butter and steaming the crabs and clams gathered in the bay. From town we had bought sweet corn and rice, fresh shrimp, and a favorite robust bread the Mexicans called *bolillos*.

Afterward, I sat by the campfire and bathed in moonlight until the group went to bed. The only sound came from the fire, the occasional flatulent staccato of burning sapwood. The absence of wind kept the surf completely still. The sea crept toward me silently, its frothy fingers reaching for the sea refuse above the tide line. I slipped into my sleeping bag, feeling an uncomfortable coldness on the sand.

Beneath a shrimp-pink dawn, as Edward Hoagland says, my students gathered on the rocks above our last low tide. Holding Jessica in my arms, I joined them to stare quietly across the ever-widening Gulf. Only eighty miles distant, the Baja peninsula inched away from me, but it was as if I were across the water slipping off with the land mass. Behind us, Terry, Karen, and Erica's parents finished packing the trucks and van.

The susurration of the ocean called to me while I contemplated lava and sand, mud flats and tide pools, attempting to make sense of my divided feelings for this region of desert and sea, and for the desert and sea within me. I had little desire to return to my other reality, my calling to mortgages and moil. I wanted to remain in this in-between place open to mountains and sky and yet hidden with unexpected wonders. I wanted the excitement and richness of oceans rather than the tedium and poverty of deserts.

The sea was a place of excess, of twice-daily renewal, where every turn of a stone uncovered something pulsating and vibrant. The desert, on the other hand, was so exposed, its edges so hard. Life there meant hunkering down and cloistering oneself. It meant making sacrifices. The desert was a place of seclusion where you confronted your demons, a place of hermits and holy men. And I was neither.

fear of snakes

They live in the desert, which means, undoubtedly, I live with them. Snakes. All kinds: pale, wormlike blind snakes; coral snakes, dressed for Halloween to advertise their poison; six-foot constrictors called bull snakes; and rattlesnakes, lots of rattlesnakes. Of these, we have westerns, western diamondbacks, sidewinders, tigers, blacktails, Mohaves and Hopis, pygmies, speckleds, and Arizona blacks. And this doesn't include the numerous hybrids and subspecies. The Sonoran Desert is rattlesnake paradise or, depending on your point of view, rattlesnake hell.

When the weather warms in February or March, I usually begin to see rattlesnakes, rippling across roads, laid out in a smudge of sunlight, sometimes even curled up on my porch like Samson's severed locks. Or I'll stumble upon them—rattles whirring—while walking among the bursage and paloverde. Ann Zwinger says rattlesnakes are the desert's caffeine. But being hypersensitive to their presence doesn't lessen the thrill of an encounter—it's like the rush of an illicit affair.

Above: Diamondback rattlesnake *(Crotalus atrox)*

I admit that I don't fear snakes as I should. It's an attraction. I'm drawn to their differentness, their exothermic, vermiform, scaly bodies and lidless eyes. I like snakes *up close*, next to my skin; sometimes I carry them in pockets like loose change or draped around my neck like avant-garde jewelry. Their allure rises from my earliest memories, from a malachite-scaled racer that came to me across the grass when I was six years old. We lived in a duplex at Travis Air Force Base near Sacramento—103 Norton Street, I remember. After my mother found me with the snake, she ran to the house across the driveway and told our neighbor something like, "Quick, there's a snake in my yard!" He appeared barefoot, wearing only shorts, a garden hoe locked in both hands. "No!" I cried. "Let it go! Let it go!" I pounded my balled fists against the backs of his thighs as he trapped it against our house and hacked at it over and over. My mother pulled me away, but later I lifted the lid to the garbage can and watched its lacerated segments twist and slide along the blood-streaked aluminum walls, hoping that it would live and escape. From then on I stopped showing snakes to my mother.

Like the rattlesnake I found when I was ten years old and living in Tucson. Someone had killed it—I don't remember who or why—but I found its head. Its skin felt cool, smooth, and resilient where it dilated around a pair of swollen poison glands. Its eyes, liquid beads with slitted pupils, were clear, alive. I pried the mouth open, exposing its white, cottonlike flesh and a double row of tiny, curved teeth. Two fangs, neatly folded into the upper jaw, lay tucked against slight mounds of tissue. I stuck in my finger and lifted one translucent hypodermic, swinging it forward into striking position. And then it disappeared, its quarter-inch length slipping into my fingertip.

I squeezed and sucked as much fluid out of the wound as possible and spent the rest of the day in bed, nauseous. I didn't tell anyone. I was afraid I was dead already, although I now know it was only fear that made me sick. I'm fortunate to have escaped even an infection. But at the time I had heard all the stories about rattlesnake bites, tales enhanced with vivid medical descriptions of cut-and-suck and self-amputation and punctuated with death tolls (a dozen or so every year in the United

States). One story in particular played out before me—the one about a cowboy who survived a rattlesnake strike unbitten but died after removing his boots later on. The snake had pierced the stiff leather of one of his boots with its fangs and left them there as a deadly gift.

I once allowed a Sonoran mountain kingsnake to bite me 147 times. It was summer camp, I was a counselor, and crazy stunts seemed part of the job. At least I wasn't ridiculed, and at nineteen, lean and bronzed, I could be excused for anything—any amount of mental disturbance. For three days I counted the bites, one after another after another, until dozens became scores, impressing my camper charges with my nerve as the snake repeatedly wrapped its needlelike teeth around my knuckles, flattening out its entire head as it unlocked its jaws and worked its mouth as if trying to swallow my hand. It was a curious display, no more painful than my tetanus booster, and I felt wild and powerful in my control of it. I bled only a little.

That same summer I collected a diamondback rattlesnake with my ungloved hands while it slept among its coils. Normally, I would have pinned its head with a stick before gripping it by the neck, but I had an audience to impress. I remember how the snake's muscular helix twisted loose in my hands and my sudden anxiety as its fangs unfolded and a spasm forced an ejaculation of sticky poison down my left forearm. What do you do when you're *that* intimate with a four-foot viper? I couldn't drop it and run. I couldn't ask for help. I was committed, and should have been institutionalized. Afterwards, I believed I would never again be so bold when I encountered a rattlesnake, audience or none. Sure. I also believed that the man who can caress a rattlesnake can do anything.

Years ago, when we were living in Mesa, Arizona, where I was teaching science, my wife and I walked the trail to the Wind Cave in Usery Mountain Park. It was our first visit there together, and I think that if we had remained in Mesa, the short trail up old Scar Face would have become our favorite place for day hikes. That early spring of 1986, as the earth listed toward equinox, the winter annuals had just begun to flower, splattering the desert with lavender and gold. The scent of wet creosote, together with the ratcheting of cactus wrens and the E-note whistles of curve-billed thrashers, garnished the air. It felt good to be out of the house on a Saturday morning as warm as blood. We dressed for fair weather—shorts and T-shirts. No boots, just hiking shoes, which crunched softly on ground textured like vermiculite. I carried our lunch in a canvas knapsack. Karen carried a plastic water bottle in her hand.

The outing was Karen's idea: something simple and romantic, she'd thought, to deepen our marriage of five years. I confess now that I needed to attend to her more, that I had been distant, focused more on my students—especially the one who was baby-sitting for us that day. Karen and I already had two small girls, Jessica and Kasondra, and very soon—soon after we beat the crowds to the Wind Cave, in fact—she would become pregnant with our third, Melissa. Somehow, I had missed what was important. Karen wanted me to pursue her, to study her. She wanted me to discover the intricacies of *her* nature, what special environment made her feel comfortable and secure, what temperature and humidity and nourishment encouraged her to thrive in our marriage. Instead, I focused more on nurturing other interests.

I knew a lot about rattlesnakes. I had kept several species in my classroom for years. Karen, however, hated it—not the snakes or my interest in their poisonous nature but my fraternization with them. She knew it was foolish to play with danger and to be so casual about it, as I was (probably one of the reasons she studied emergency medicine). When a young diamondback rattlesnake appeared in our yard one evening, Karen became angry with me after I began prodding it with a shovel, intending to carry it into the desert away from the house. The snake acted strangely lethargic, refusing to rattle even as I caught it, gripping its head with one hand while its body entwined the other. Karen, seeing this, swore at me in the darkness, following me at a distance all the way to where I finally released it. She remained upset for hours, unmollified by my explanation that I was simply caring for a defenseless, confused creature. "I wasn't sure you would make it back home," she told me afterward.

It's ironic that Karen once asked me for a snake instead of an engagement ring. The snake's name was Molasses, a four-foot Colombian red-tailed boa constrictor that a friend of mine needed to sell. Karen loved him the first time she held him, the weight of Molasses lying across her shoulders, his flanks pressing against her breasts. "He's smiling at me," she said, noticing the upward curl of the reptile's lips. "I think he likes me too." Seeing her pleasure and fearlessness, I thought she should have him. In desiring the captive boa constrictor, Karen had stepped closer to me, closer to possessing me. But Karen wanted a tamed snake, and I never got around to buying it for her.

People had massed at the Wind Cave trailhead: Boy Scouts and groups of winter visitors. License plates in the parking lot announced the visitors' origins: Minnesota, North Dakota, Saskatchewan, Alberta. Every year they'd come, retired couples in their campers and travel trailers, escaping the cold northern climate to invade our parks and monuments and congest our streets. We called them "snowbirds"; nearby Apache Junction, a seasonal trailer town, was their winter haven.

Karen and I quickly outpaced the crowds, stretching our legs on the steep trail. Along with the lupine and gold poppy and the creosote bushes, bursage, prickly pear and barrel cacti peppered the rocky slopes. The spider-legged branches of ocotillo had flushed with leaves, and pantomiming saguaros stood poised in half-told gossip. Below us, the desert dropped away and flattened into serpentine patterns of arroyos. Overhead rose thousand-foot cliffs of welded tuff, a fusion of once-hot volcanic ash from a leftover burp of the same processes that created the nearby Superstition Mountains some fifteen to thirty million years ago. "Scar Face," what locals called Pass Mountain, got its name from a single jagged blaze of ocher that split the darker stratified layers. Our destination lay where slope and cliff met: a water- and gravity-formed seam—the Wind Cave.

We had hiked for half a mile when, above the first switchbacks, an explosive, buzzing sound stopped us. Across the trail, three or four feet from Karen's naked legs, a huge diamondback rattlesnake rested in the sun. I looked up at Karen, who had pushed on ahead of me but now stared at me with an expression that said, *Don't even think about it!* "Don't move!" I said. She didn't. She didn't even speak. I crept closer and the snake's warning began to stutter, its rattle—more than a dozen segments—only twitching. Slowly, the reptile slid off the trail into the cover of a prickly pear cactus and quit rattling altogether.

A few boys in khaki scout uniforms joined us. The snake remained among the spiny pads of the cactus, allowing us to watch it more closely, close enough to see individual scales and the imbricated pattern they made, like miniature Spanish tiles set in elastic mortar. I could just make out the sensory pits at the end of its snout: a heat-seeking guidance system for targeting warm blooded mammals. Two-tenths of a degree's difference in the ambient temperature is enough. Even in total darkness the snake's infrared "vision" could pick us out. "Diamondback," I told the group, slipping into my teaching mode. "It's probably just out of hibernation, looking for a nice rock to warm up on before going hunting."

I moved off the trail to get closer to the rattlesnake. More people gathered to see what had drawn our attention, and I was aware of them. I wanted to catch it. To show off. Then someone appeared at my side, a tall man with white hair and a cream-colored polo shirt whom I'd seen at the parking lot. "Diamondback rattlesnake," I said again. "I found it on the trail." The man said nothing. As I bent again toward the snake, out of the corner of my eye I noticed something incongruent. A gray arm, extended. Yellow surgical tubing pulled taut. I turned, suddenly realizing what it was. I had hardly opened my mouth to shout when he released the steel ball. A dull crack, and the snake began rolling over and over, thrashing wildly among the pads of the prickly pear, its head crushed by an old man with a slingshot.

I could taste the bitterness rising in me but no words came. Ignoring me, he stepped around me to strike the snake again. I stood, transfixed in place. His wife cowered behind him, her arms held tightly against her white blouse. "Be careful," she said. "I got him," he reassured her and then fired another ball in one quick movement. "He's dead."

I'd seen this kind of human behavior before, and I knew what he was doing. He thought he was Saint George slaying the dragon, protecting us, protecting me, from a menace. In his mind it deserved to die. The snake, the embodiment of evil, a detestable creature since the fall of man, the *serpent* who seduced Eve and then had sex with her, bringing sin into the world, was in conflict with people. The trespasser didn't belong in our garden. But this was *my* home; the county park was *my backyard!* I wanted to knock the old man down and wrap the slingshot around his neck. Karen, however, pulled me away. "Let's go," she said. "It's over. There's nothing you can do."

Farther up the trail, the desert seemed less vibrant. Colors had dimmed to matte gray; birds were silent. I looked back one time. People stood around the man, who had bent to his knees and was hacking with his penknife at the snake's rattles—his Arizona trophy. His glory only illuminated more my own defeat. I felt a sudden loss, as if he had killed some part of me and was now cutting it away. The snake was mine; he had taken it from me. Yet, I felt shame, too. Like that green racer when I was six, I had participated in its death. My attraction to the rattlesnake had drawn attention to its presence. My affair with it had drawn the steel ball. "There's nothing you can do," Karen repeated, but I had already done too much, gone too far. Shame *and* loss. The world was all wrong. I should have been angry still, but I was afraid.

old hat gulch

A few miles south of Oracle, Arizona, near the dirt track of the old Mt. Lemmon Highway, a cattle guard marks the entrance to the YMCA Triangle Y Ranch Camp. When we arrived there in 1986, during the fore-summer drought of late May, the northern slopes of the Santa Catalina Mountains still retained the chlorophylls of spring. Mesquite trees and netleaf hackberry shone with bright leaves. Fierce catclaw mimosa shrubs seemed tame behind their green cloaks. The air smelled like stirred earth. An afternoon sun burned, and every plant shimmered in light reflected from suspended dust. Soft clicks and buzzes announced the presence of infatuated insects—adult grasshoppers, beetles, cicadas—vying for female affections.

Our arrival at the YMCA camp always carried with it certain feelings of nostalgia. Since Karen and I had met and fallen in love there in 1979, and later exchanged marriage vows in the camp chapel and took perma-

---

Above: Immature Cooper's hawk *(Accipiter cooperii)*

nent positions as program directors, camp had become entwined with our lives. Every back road, trail, rustic building, scrub-clotted hill, and labyrinthine arroyo preserved seasons of memories. More than our place in Mesa, Arizona, this high desert camp was home.

The Triangle Y Ranch Camp originally was the home of Elizabeth Lambert Wood. In 1902, when she was thirty years old, she came to Oracle with her ophthalmologist husband, William Lee Wood. "The Doctor," as she liked to call him, was suffering from tuberculosis and had decided that the warm, dry southwestern climate would be best for his health. Elizabeth agreed.

After arriving in Tucson (where Elizabeth, writing to a friend, said she couldn't find a single Bible!), the couple rode for six and a half hours by four-horse stage to Oracle and the popular Mountain View Hotel. There they remained for the next two years, making friends with the local people, visiting with guests at the rival Arcadia Ranch Hotel, playing host to prospectors, and taking daily horseback rides. Their two children, eight-year-old Lambert Alexander and six-year-old Helen Henrietta, also soon joined them.

As the Doctor's health improved, the Woods traveled back to their home in Portland, Oregon. But they had fallen in love with Oracle and returned every winter. Over the years the two became popular figures among the area's mining camps. As caretakers, they lived on several properties, including a mill at Peppersauce Canyon and Charley Brajevich's three-room cabin in Southern Belle Canyon. They became close friends to William "Buffalo Bill" and Lulu Cody during the days of the Cody-Dyer mining operations at nearby Campo Bonito. Elizabeth spent many afternoons on the porch of the Mountain View Hotel with Lulu Cody, and one of her greatest impressions of that time she records in her later writings as if she were exposing some secret: Elizabeth had learned from Lulu that Buffalo Bill's long white hair was actually a wig. But it wasn't until after World War I that the Woods permanently settled in Oracle. Tragically, their son Lambert was dead. In the summer of 1918, he was killed in action while commanding a machine gun company of the 9th Infantry in France. He was twenty-three. When the Southern Belle properties came on the market, Elizabeth, without consulting her husband, who was very sick, offered ten thousand dollars for them. The offer was low, half as much as what was being asked, but she managed the deal. Charley's cabin, Southern Belle and Morning Star mines, the mill site at Peppersauce, and the Castro Ranch called the Crooked G all belonged to the Woods. William was pleased with his wife's boldness, but unfortunately, he never lived long enough to fully enjoy owning the land he loved. He died shortly afterward in 1923.

After her husband died, Elizabeth moved from Charley's cabin in Southern Belle Canyon to her Peppersauce property. "The large spring running in a stream through the place under a natural grove of sycamores, black walnuts and ash trees encourages the cultivation of flowers and shrubs," she wrote while living there, describing how she cherished a wild columbine growing along the stream and collected its seed to scatter on its banks. "It is a magnificent sight."

When her daughter Helen died in 1925 following an illness after giving birth, Elizabeth adopted her grandson and gave him her son's name, Lambert Alexander. Together they raised cattle and a few horses on the Crooked G Ranch in the Old Hat Mining District, where the YMCA camp now sits, until he, too, was killed in action during World War II. In the camp's dining hall, framed photographs of both sons hang on opposite sides of the wooden doors, the men wearing the uniforms they died in. Across many summers I had stared into their eyes, wondering who they were, what they were like, knowing only that they were Elizabeth's children and that she had raised them to be courageous men.

Over the next decades Elizabeth operated her ranch and her mines alone, receiving royalties for profits made by Idaho mining engineer E. J. Ewing and later by the Mountain Mining and Milling Company, and writing for magazines and for children. Her affection for children was evident not only in her stories but also in her financial generosity. In 1939 she donated her Peppersauce property to the Salvation Army for its Camp O'Wood. (In 1992, the Salvation Army turned the deed over to the Arizona Boy's Ranch, who use the site as a "boot camp" for problem juveniles, continuing Elizabeth's legacy to children.) In 1948, she donated her

Crooked G Ranch above Old Hat Gulch to the YMCA of Tucson, who renamed it the Triangle Y Ranch Camp. She lived on this property first in what is now the recreation hall and later in what became the camp caretaker's home until her death in 1963.

The recreation hall is still one of my favorite buildings at camp. There's history written into its hodgepodge construction, a result of successive improvements over the years as it grew to accommodate a popular youth camp. The hall itself was once the open courtyard of a three-room house, until a ramada covered it along with its stone retaining wall. Later, wooden sidings were added to enclose the structure and then concrete floors. More than seventy years ago, in a short, roughly typed manuscript titled "A Sketch of the Life of Elizabeth Lambert Wood," she wrote, "If you have not experienced it you cannot know what a privilege and joy it is to see your own brand on cattle and horses as you ride the country over on your own good horse." These words she followed with a tiny ink drawing of her brand. Today, burned into the stained oak planks inside the recreation hall, you can still see it: a cookie-cutter bell hanging from a horizontal S—Southern "Belle."

The novelist and essayist David James Duncan says that we all, eventually, become natives of our places—we have to, in order to remain alive. Southern Belle Canyon, Peppersauce Canyon, and Old Hat Gulch with their cabins and mines and ranches were Elizabeth's home for most of her life. She remained there into her nineties, surviving her husband, two children, and a grandchild, quietly writing her stories and children's books. Reading her letters and stories now, I get a glimpse of the "privilege and joy" she speaks of. As it had become mine, Elizabeth had made the landscape her own, and I believe the place helped carry her through the emotionally devastating periods in her life. In her words, she would not willingly exchange her home for any other place in the world. I had shared her sentiments, as I shared some deep connection with her—one that seemed even closer than the obvious similarity between our names. But too soon I would willingly discard those feelings as well as any affinity we might have had. Elizabeth had been the mother of heroes.

Since the summer of 1949 when the Triangle Y Ranch Camp began operating as a boys' camp, the facilities grew from a single building (the recreation hall) and some tents to a complex organization involving seventy professional staff, fifty buildings spread out over 140 acres, and more than a thousand children—boys and girls—over eight weeks of summer. Ownership of the Southern Belle claims also transferred to the YMCA along with the Crooked G Ranch property. The camp used Charley Brajevich's cabin location, renamed the Outpost, as an overnight camping area where older children learned campcraft skills, outdoor cooking, minimal impact camping, and gold panning. (Although prospectors have played out the claims, some lucky children occasionally find gold in the tiny creek at Southern Belle Canyon near the Outpost. One summer, a boy discovered a five-eighth's-ounce nugget in the bottom of his pan . . . enough gold to pay for another week at camp.) The Triangle Y's principal activities, however, included horseback riding and wrangling, nature and environmental education, swimming, arts and crafts, archery, and riflery.

I first came to the Triangle Y as a twelve-year-old camper, returning there as a counselor during my college years. In consecutive seasons I worked as a senior counselor, nature director, and finally the program director, responsible for staff supervision and the overall camp program management. Karen, among her other duties such as relief nurse and cook, trained young, would-be counselors.

The summer of 1986 was the last season we worked at the Triangle Y Ranch Camp. Karen, three months pregnant with Melissa, and I lived with our two small daughters in a private trailer just above the recreation hall and adjacent to Elizabeth Wood's former home. Our summer began with spending part of an early June afternoon unloading furnishings and boxes of clothes from our truck, cleaning the trailer (and evicting a family of spotted skunks from under the kitchen sink), turning on the electricity and gas, and refitting the evaporative cooler. Later, we took a break from settling in, and I walked down the main road past the athletic field toward the eastern border of the property, following a path that Elizabeth Wood may have walked on similar afternoons. Living and working in an environment that suffused me with nature normally diminished the weight of my job responsibilities. Although I was really only moving from one teaching job to another, at least in the camp "classroom," escape was only a short trek in any direction. And, more and more, I craved escape.

After scrambling down a soft bank at the far end of the athletic field, I joined a channel of fine quartz sand that bisected the camp from east to west: Old Hat Gulch. Between a corrugation of low hills, the arroyo created a passageway for wildlife through thickets of catclaw and hackberry. Animals like javelina and kit foxes, and even mountain lions occasionally left a calligraphy of tracks in the soft substrate as they traveled along the wildlife funnel. Less noticeable were imprinted messages of smaller creatures—kangaroo rats and whiptail lizards—that had recently found the vegetation a convenient place to forage or seek shade and cover. Old Hat Gulch, which parted the landscape as my emotions had begun to divide me, was one place I often disappeared to that last summer at camp.

Downstream, the channel narrowed; the banks rose to my shoulders. The enclosing walls of silt, curtains of vegetation, and sandy carpet snatched sound from the air. To speak seemed a violation of natural law. In that place, I might encounter anything: cellophane-winged wasps prowling for spiders in the undergrowth, blister beetles in their medieval coat-of-arms, or a nest of Cooper's hawks in a large hackberry, like the nest several seasons before that had launched me into the sport of falconry.

That earlier summer, a sharp *kek kek kek* drew my attention to the uppermost branches of a tree where a female Cooper's hawk warned me not to intrude. I did anyway. Her nest, a platform of sticks and bark, stood out against the green foliage, and although I couldn't see inside the nest, I guessed that at least one fledgling occupied it. Directly beneath it, lay an array of refuse—feathers, bones, and the desiccated leg of a nest mate.

I knew that with many birds of prey, especially those with large broods, nature adjusts the number of offspring according to the abundance of quarry. In Cooper's hawks there is a relationship between food and fratricide. The hawks lay eggs as much as four days apart, staggering their hatching dates, so older siblings can prey on the younger if the need arises. Cannibalism allows a rapid adjustment to food availability, ensuring that at least one young family member survives.

Cooper's hawks like to hunt in dense growth. Short, powerful wings help them to accelerate and maneuver between branches, "recklessly" plunging into thick brush in pursuit of prey. Broken feathers are not uncommon. A long, flexible, rudderlike tail provides the flight stability for this twist and dodge and pounce method of hunting, one reason the birds make an exciting subject for falconers.

I loved to watch Cooper's hawks hunt along the arroyo, silently gliding along the course of the dry wash and repeatedly rushing toward cover, a tactic to dislodge their quarry. The hawk's most common strategy, however, was still-hunting—using concealment rather than silent flight and flush. From a perch hidden among the limbs of a tree, the raptor would scan the woodland, listening for the call of its prey, like the song of a mourning dove or drumming of a roadrunner. Once the hawk had its prey in sight, it would fly above the animal, side-slip into a short dive, and then pin it to the ground. The velocity of the hawk and the sudden thrusting of its talons produced a strike shock I could actually hear.

I had to have one. Since reading *My Side of the Mountain* when I was a teenager, I had wanted to fly hawks at game, to be a falconer. When I climbed that tree in the arroyo and peered into the Cooper's nest I found the opportunity—the fledgling bolted from its nest on unpracticed wings and I captured it. By the end of that summer, the two of us were hunting quail together, although both were illegal—taking quail out of season and hunting with a hawk. In subsequent years, as a licensed falconer, I would bring my hawks to camp with me every summer, finding a kind of refuge in the solitude of quiet afternoons flying my birds. My last summer was different, however, for at the end of the school year, I had returned to the wild a favorite Harris' hawk I'd hunted with for years, handing the bird to a favorite student for her to release. I must have known, thinking about it now, that soon I would no longer care about hawks or practicing falconry.

Farther downstream, the vines of a canyon grape entangled an elderberry tree. The single grape vine, with its wide, maplelike leaves, tendril coils, and shedding bark was the only one of its kind that I was aware of outside of Campo Bonito three miles to the west. Since it rarely grew away from permanent water, the vine probably was a leftover from a time, before mining in the valley lowered the water table, when the arroyo in Old Hat Gulch was a perennial stream.

Along the dry wash, sprawling catclaw, invaders from the higher woodlands, bore hooks of malicious intentions. The mimosa, also called the wait-a-minute bush because of its tenacious "claws," was the scourge of camp. Even when pruned to the ground, the catclaw soon recovered, reaching out along roadsides and across trails to harass bare-legged hikers, particularly at night. Karen discovered the plant her first summer when she rushed through a thicket in the dark. The shrubs tore away her shirt and left a tattoo pattern of parallel tracks on her back. I, however, never learned respect for it and often returned from my nighttime forays with bloodied arms and legs.

An elderly hackberry tree offered me a place to rest at the eastern property line, so I climbed its branches and dissolved into the gray foliage. From my perch I watched shadows lengthen across sand and shrub and rock, colors bleaching into one anemic tone. The landscape seemed to sigh, relieved from the aching, throbbing brilliance of sun. Ash arrived as the prominent color with the evening. The dusty hue infused everything in varying degrees, veiling the green vegetation and laying a dull film over shimmering quartz and mica. The air carried the sweet, warm scent of mistletoe, like the smell of devotion—something fresh and new, something undeserved.

Later, I strolled back to our trailer under a sky darkening from grenadine to plum. The following day, the first camp staff were due to arrive and to begin training. Thinking about it filled me with both excitement and trepidation. It would be a time of reunion with old friends and an opportunity to meet new ones. It would be a day like the one, eight years before, when Karen first got my attention, arriving late to the first ice-breaker session in skin-tight, white jeans, her long blond, Farrah Fawcett curls swept back away from her face. She was seventeen then, a counselor for our backpacking program; I was twenty and directing the program. Everyone noticed her, but in a few days we were inseparable. Then, after a cup of hot Jell-O in her cabin late one night, she kissed me (she still denies being so forward but I know it's true) and I fell hard for her. It was the beginning of a passionate romance that ended with our marriage eighteen months later.

Relationships at camp can be dynamic, enduring if only in memory. It happened when people of similar backgrounds and interests got thrown together in a place, a community really, where work was exhausting and personal privacy unknown. Façades dissolved quickly. (Karen gave up the curls for bandannas her first week.) Nothing was hidden; you were visible at your best and at your worst. At camp, hanging out your underwear in public was not a euphemism but a personal ritual. But in this we were all bound together. We had mutual needs: physical ones like hot showers, clean clothes, and days off, and emotional ones like encouragement and companionship. In a sense, camp was a commune, and we all became lovers.

She came with my invitation at the end of June, a few weeks after camp had begun that last season, and with her arrival my life came undone, as I knew it would. Perhaps it was the permanence of marriage that appalled me, that my marriage had become like the "awful and irrefutable *rock-ness*" that Peter Matthiessen faced in the Himalayas, which intensified his own feelings of transience. And perhaps, as he says some do, I responded with "greed for a few gobbets of raw experience" to dull my own sense of mortality. No, I believe I was more shallow than this, and maybe now, with these events in the past, all I'm doing is searching for some explanation greater than the obvious one: that I was purely selfish. I had already left—emotionally, anyway—my pregnant wife and my children. I had stopped eating. Instead of sleeping, I wandered frantically among the hills and trails, telling Karen that it was my job to enforce a midnight curfew, while at the same time I was violating it with someone else.

On one night just prior to her coming, I hiked out to the yucca forest, something I often enjoyed doing with Karen and friends but never alone. A gibbous moon had cast silver-black into the desert, blanching the roads. I didn't use a flashlight, and wouldn't again. In fact, soon I would start wearing all-dark clothing at night so that even in moonlight no one might see me.

When I crossed the stone bridge leading out of camp, I imagined a pair of yellow-green eyes pinning me to the darkness. I recalled what had happened to Jeff Teich there on a similar night several summers before. Jeff was the unit director for the older boys and a friend of many years. His casual personality and quirky dress—bandannas, Birkenstock sandals, and corduroy shorts—made him instantly likable. In the "off-season" he taught business at Arizona State University and loaned out living space in his Tempe apartment.

Jeff didn't see the animal but only heard it scream a warning as he approached the bridge. "It was a chilling scream, like a woman's," he said. "I stopped and ran back the other way." The next morning, I took note of his quiet concern after we found several, saucer-sized tracks in the dust. Each had a heavy center pad and four toes without claw marks. He told me that recently he had seen a large, tawny-colored animal with a long tail as it padded across the dining hall parking area.

Few people saw mountain lions anywhere those days. To have one stalking around camp seemed phenomenal. When I mentioned the possibility to John Ronquillo, the camp caretaker and long-time resident of Oracle (and friend of Elizabeth Wood), he said that less than fifty years ago cougars were common in the area. Later, I learned that wildlife officials estimate that about twenty-five hundred still haunt Arizona's roughest backcountry, and their studies indicate that lion populations are quite stable, even in places where lion persecution is the greatest.

A full grown mountain lion may weigh as much as two hundred

pounds. She will kill javelina, pronghorn, deer, livestock, and occasionally a hiker. Jeff stopped walking the trails without a flashlight. His mountain lion claims became a camp joke, especially since he began wearing a gaudy lanyard necklace clipped to a flashlight even in the middle of the day. No one believed him. No one but me. I've always wondered if the staff's jokes didn't stem from some deep unspeakable fear that one last rogue mountain lion might actually still roam those hills, that the place could actually kill the unwary . . . or foolish.

The tissuelike petals of prickly poppy lit my path at regular intervals like delicate Mexican *luminarias*. Dark green mats of fairy duster, a perennial named for its lavender plumes, bordered the road. I turned north and followed an overgrown horse trail when the road ended, and now the shadowy knobs of Arizona thistle touched my knees and thighs. After a time, a number of tall figures suddenly appeared, and then a forest of dark giants enclosed me. Individuals rose from central trunks, encased in a shaggy "bark" of matted gray leaves. The trunks supported crowns of narrow, pointed leaves that radiated outward in spiky spheres. Variations of unconformity proceeded from this basic pattern: single trunks splitting into twins and triplets, some reaching up to perpendicular heights and others surrendering to windblown angles.

Although soaptree yuccas still dotted the desert-grassland, this dense enclave of forty or so plants was a remnant that recalled better times for yuccas there. As if in defiance to their dwindling numbers, most of the plant's crowns sprouted flowering stalks, displaying closely packed, creamy blossoms whose waxy petals absorbed the moonlight. A few crowns still gripped stalks from the previous year, their woody capsules split, dried, and seedless.

I'd always admired the plants. They were like so much else I had encountered in that place, where life sometimes withdrew to pockets and yet held on, where character narrowed down to its essence. The plants were like the people there. People like Elizabeth Wood who suffered and then recovered from loss and adjusted to the changes, who stayed on the land and left a legacy to others. If I had fully understood the significance of this kind of integrity with people and their commitment to the landscape, would I have consummated the betrayal that crouched in my mind that night? The betrayal of my wife and daughters, my friends and teaching colleagues? The betrayal of my position there and my own legacy to children? I don't know. And it makes little difference. I was not in the place of understanding, only reacting.

Sitting in the yucca forest, I watched the moonlight illuminate an occasional moth, which fluttered in unwinding helixes among the flowers. I imagined that the moths seemed frenzied about their sexual task and the limited time to accomplish it. Female yucca moths pollinate all yuccas. They live for only a few days because they lack a digestive system. They starve themselves to death for sex, the moth's short but entire adult life spent on reproduction. She collects pollen from one yucca flower, packs it into a ball under her head, and then carries the ball to another flower on another plant. There, as if she "knows" exactly what she's doing, she stuffs pieces of her pollen ball into slits circling the flower's stigma, ensuring that seeds will develop. But her act is not purely unselfish, for prior to leaving, she inserts her ovipositor into the flower's ovary and lays her eggs, usually one egg to every row of future seeds. As the fat pink caterpillars grow, they eat the seeds, then bore through the pod and rappel on a silk thread to the ground, where they pupate and wait out the winter months. Adult yucca moths emerge the following year to complete the cycle.

I've heard that this behavior, refined to the degree where some species of yuccas have their own species of moths, helps the plant as well as the insect because the larvae don't eat all the seeds. The relationship between the two is a classic example of symbiosis: two different species living in intimate contact. In this case, because both species supposedly benefit, ecologists further define the symbiosis, calling it mutualism. But parasitism is also a kind of symbiosis. Not all relationships (particularly ones involving sex) are mutually beneficial. One member or the other usually owns the greater risk. Yuccas also reproduce without flowers, without sex, a more "primitive" form of propagation (a regression in response to seed-eating larvae?), but one that doesn't require pollen-balling moths.

Perhaps what some see as mutualism is only an evolutionary reaction to parasitism. Certainly, the moth gets more out of the affair.

I stayed out in the yucca forest until after midnight, moon shadow sharpening the edges of stones, and Mars rising as a burning punctuation mark on the ecliptic, on my life. I had decisions to make; instead, I would allow others to make them for me. On a nearby ridge, coyotes were speaking in tongues, mourning some loss, or some predestined allotment handed out by the universe.

twin ponds

On one of the hottest, driest, most skin-cracking days in early July 1986, I reluctantly agreed to help Terry Hutchins with stocking his man-made pond. Terry, the camp's nature director, was eternally enthusiastic about his program. Normally taciturn and impenetrable, the sandy-headed junior high science teacher degenerated into a long-haired, unshaven "nature freak" at camp. His own students wouldn't have recognized him without his pressed pants and tie. But at the Triangle Y Ranch Camp, my best friend was teaching science, outdoors.

From the first day of staff training to the last session with the children, camp emphasized environmental education. We taught our staff, who were mostly young college students, to demonstrate an ecological awareness in all activities, to do no harm toward anyone or anything. Whether it was exercising minimal impact on camp-outs, cleaning up trails and cabin areas, appreciating wildlife and each other, or simply conserving

Above: Backswimmer (family Notonectidae)

water while washing, one of our purposes was to instill in young minds a respect for all life.

Terry's nature program focused on teaching these values. He had constructed greenhouses, gardens, beehives, solar cookers, incubators, nature trails and games, together with scores of static displays and hands-on projects to put nature within the grasp of children. Now, he wanted me to hike three miles in 104 degrees to a pair of stock tanks called Twin Ponds to collect aquatic wildlife for an aquarium and pond, carrying buckets, nets, and jars across a stretch of mesquite and prickly pear desert. My reluctance stemmed from more than just the physical heat.

Twin Ponds was one of our favorite places near camp, the only place where you might find water all year, even in summer. And water in the desert draws wildlife. The ponds, a construction of Dean Prichard, a local rancher and historian, filled a drainage where two successive earthen dams held seasonal runoff. The upper pond, once filled, spilled into the lower, which fed the roots of a giant cottonwood. Aside from attracting birds and deer, javelina and mountain lions, the ponds themselves were home to an array of diving insects, canyon tree frogs, and snakes. Cattails frayed the water's edge, while duckweed and algae carpeted its surface. Twin Ponds, in harmonic duet, bubbled and cooed and trilled with life.

Our trail took us through knobs of Precambrian rock known as Oracle granite. The outcrops, which erosion once loosened from the core of a mountain, continued to decompose, a process that converts angular blocks into rounded boulders. Exposed to moisture and seasonal freezing and thawing, the rocks' surfaces peeled away in thin sheets like dying rose petals. The house-sized boulders domed several hills and resembled giant petrified eggs standing erect in nests of scrub vegetation. Some of these boulders, Terry had discovered earlier, had excellent surfaces from which to teach rappelling, one of his more popular activities.

I was sweating freely, my heart pounding in my ears and my face red by the time I thought I could smell the water of Twin Ponds. I tried to convince myself that thirst favors the desert's aesthetics. We had neglected to bring water with us, and I didn't care to drink from the tanks and risk the flesh-wasting symptoms of *Giardia,* an intestinal parasite associated with water and cattle. Terry had already learned about the parasite the hard way, incapacitated on a backpacking trip while "running at both ends," as he put it.

I considered detouring farther west into the hills for water. Through the dust-haze, I occasionally caught sight of High Jinks, once the cabin of the legendary William F. "Buffalo Bill" Cody, and now the home of Dean Prichard. Dean, who sometimes dressed as Buffalo Bill and rode horseback in La Fiesta de los Vaqueros, Tucson's annual rodeo parade, had preserved part of the original cabin—a sitting room with wood-beam ceilings, a stone fireplace, antique furniture, photos, and other relics—in honor of the western entertainer. High Jinks is on the National Registry of Historic Places.

Terry and I didn't know it then, but in a few years Dean Prichard would cut a new trail from Oracle Ridge past his place at High Jinks to the American Flag Ranch (built around 1877) just southeast of Twin Ponds. The Arizona Trail. It would become Arizona's signature path, linking Mexico to Utah with 750 miles of desert and mountain trails, which hiking enthusiasts like Dean would complete over the next decade. Terry liked checking off trails on his topographic maps. He'd already hiked most of the routes in Grand Canyon, some of them with me. We may have walked the length of the Arizona Trail together, too, if I had made other choices that summer. It was something I would think a lot about in the years to come.

I should have known better. Traveling in the desert after eight in the morning during summer can be hazardous, with or without water. I learned this one year in Pima Canyon, north of Tucson when I was fourteen. I had run away from home over an emotional breakup with my first girlfriend. My best friend Dale accompanied me. I knew we'd find water in the canyon, so I had brought only one canteen for both of us. It was empty before we arrived at the trailhead. More arrogant than cautious, I pushed on, hiking farther and farther into the canyon. Whenever Dale voiced his concern, which was rapidly becoming distress, I told him we should find water just around the next turn. He was too inexperienced not to believe me. What I didn't tell him was that we had already passed, in my estimation, the point of no return. We had to find water because the hike back out would kill us.

When we finally located one tiny stagnant pool, we were beyond caring about its purity. We were queasy and near exhausted—even the pebbles we had sucked on to generate saliva seemed to draw fluid from our bodies. We didn't skim away the algae mat before plunging our faces into the warm soup. Only later, after we had half-drained the pool, did we remove the scum, horsehair worms, floating insect parts, and a dead garter snake before filling our canteen. That time, I was lucky not to have seriously hurt my friend, but it seems the only wisdom I gained from the experience was discovering that green is also a texture and flavor.

Above the trail to Twin Ponds, the sun was a metallic blister. Banners of heat weighed down on me and blurred my vision. Black gnats stole fluid from the corners of my eyes and whined around my ears like atomic nuclei. Swatting at them was futile and the effort expensive. Neither Terry nor I spoke. Was it the heat or something else? Terry didn't seem to be sweating. Our friendship had been strained lately, although I didn't fully recognize this at the time. Toward the end of the last school year, I had started acting closer to the age of my students, leaving the responsibility of discipline and order to Terry on every science club activity away from the classroom. Now, at camp, I had hired one of my students as a special program assistant, a student Terry found disruptive to the club and to camp; he couldn't understand my interest in her. He must have suspected that her arrival wasn't entirely benign.

Terry wanted me to say something, I'm sure, to explain myself, to at least attempt to set our friendship right. And I should have, but this new relationship had already passed beyond its own point of no return, and to backtrack would have killed me, or so I believed. Instead, Terry and I walked in silence. Under our feet, grass was explosively brittle; other vegetation hung limp, dust-laden. No bird sang, except for the occasional furtive coo of an overheated mourning dove. Overhead, a column of turkey vultures boiled over the rim of a thermal and spilled northward. The heat could have driven a man to sinlessness—any man, that is, but me.

At the turn of last century, art historian and desert sojourner John Van Dyke wrote: "The life of the desert lives only by virtue of adapting itself to the conditions of the desert. Nature does not bend the elements to favor the plants and animals; she makes the plants and animals do the bending." Being relative newcomers to hot, arid conditions, humans are not as "bent" as some desert creatures. That day, I was sweating it—2 1/2 pounds of liquid every hour just to maintain a tolerable body temperature. Although I wasn't aware of the exact numbers, I understood the consequences if I didn't replenish the liquid. At my weight (160 pounds), losing 3 to 6 pounds of sweat would cause some discomfort—cottonmouth, flushed skin, loss of appetite. Nothing to worry about. Sweating 12 to 16 pounds would have been more alarming, causing symptoms I'd experienced before on a science club backpacking trip in the Grand Canyon: swollen tongue, salivary gland failure, slurred speech, and mental impairment. (Afterward, Karen said that I was already "mentally impaired" for forgetting to bring water in the first place. The truth is, I had given all my water to the same student now working for us at camp.) It was close. The core of my body was overheating. Critical meltdown.

Then, like now, I was not adapting well to my life in the desert, to my marriage, to my family and friendships. The blame could fall only on me. A few weeks after our hike to Twin Ponds, I would leave on my day off and never return to camp. I would abandon everyone to pursue an illicit affair. After my arrest, Terry pushed aside his own anger and pain to stay connected with me. While I was free on bond before my trial, he traveled hundreds of miles—I had retreated to another city—to meet with me. I had betrayed him, too, but he only expressed concern for me. And although I would break his trust again by using him while I was on bond to attempt to continue the affair, he never abandoned me. He patiently waited for me to come to my senses, which I eventually did. After I went to prison, Terry wrote letters and visited me on weekends. He sent lesson plans and basic science activities to use in the prison classroom where I worked as a teacher's aide. He remained close to my wife and to my children. I could give nothing in return, however, and our friendship found it impossible to bear the changes in our lives. It wouldn't survive half my sentence.

When we arrived at Twin Ponds, the upper tank was gone, its water abandoned to dry air. What had been wet and alive now stunk of death, and its odor—like my own—clung to me. The only sound was the Doppler buzz of flies. From the earthen dam, I looked at the thick, drying mud, cracked and curled like pottery sherds, filling the depression, and I felt despair. Here and there, small rotting carcasses lay, those with lungs caught by the sticky mud as they searched for a drink, those with gills caught as the margins of the last pools imploded upon them. A cluster of tracks, each imprint shaped like a fractured heart, punctuated the mud where a herd of about thirty animals had recently come for water.

Pronghorn? I thought, more hopeful than realistic. Pronghorn would have been a good omen for me. The tawny, antelopelike animals once dotted the bajadas and valleys all around the Santa Catalina Mountains. But as early as 1936, the *Tucson Daily Citizen* was reporting their decline. An article dated September 21 of that year says that in 1899 a hunter had killed a world record animal near Tucson, its horns measuring twenty inches with a sixteen-inch spread. Only four decades later, the article continues, pronghorn had become the rarest North American game species next to bighorn sheep. In the early part of last century, predation and loss of habitat had led to the near-extinction of pronghorn, animals that previously may have outnumbered buffalo.

By 1940, a small herd of Chihuahuan pronghorn still grazed north of Oracle near Twin Ponds. Witnesses counted fourteen, but the estimates ran as high as forty adults. Over the next few years, the Arizona Game and Fish Department tried to supplement these, releasing four in 1943 and another fifteen in 1945, but the results were disappointing. The transplanted animals could not adapt and died out within a decade, probably due to brush invasion of the former grassland. The Game and Fish gave up on pronghorn for the area.

The tracks at Twin Ponds could not have been pronghorn, as much as I wanted them to be. Terry identified them as javelina—we'd seen and hunted them there before.

It was smell that had helped Terry and me locate this javelina herd the last time. Since javelina, a piglike mammal but no more related to pigs than to hippopotamuses, mark areas by rubbing their breastlike, dorsal scent glands on rocks and vegetation—glands that secrete a foul-smelling oil the animals can forcefully eject when threatened—it's usually obvious where javelina bed down. Not far from Twin Ponds, we found an outcrop of boulders on a low hill with freshly disturbed soil and their pervasive skunklike odor. We returned that evening, climbed onto the rocks, and waited. Within an hour they came, wheezing and snuffling as they stepped along the hillside on their way to feed in the prickly pear and mesquite below us. I killed two of them.

Basically tropical animals, javelina were almost unheard of in the Southwest before the 1900s. Their bones are conspicuously absent from archaeological digs of Native American hearths and middens. But with the advent of cattle, the subsequent shrinkage of grasslands due to over-grazing, and the expansion of mesquite and cacti, javelina have invaded from Mexico to exploit the new habitat. The animal's fondness for prick-ly pear and mesquite beans is probably why their numbers have been increasing over the last hundred years.

Javelina and pronghorn: both New World relatives in the even-toed, hoofed clan, both southwestern brothers. The javelina, however, had accommodated itself to fit this place, even expanding its range, living side by side with coyote and coatimundi, sidewinder and saguaro. The javelina had become the charming "desert pig," while the pronghorn could never even disown its foreign misnomer of "antelope." One had made the desert its home; the other had not. I could not escape the sym-bolism. Kindred spirits may share common ground and even blood, but it's *behavior* that decides the kind of relationship they have.

On the opposite side of the earthen dam splitting Twin Ponds, cattails gagged a dead streamlet that once emptied into the second pond. But just beyond the cattails, a flat black oval, pressed up against a smaller earth-work, mirrored blue sky. Water! We scrambled down the slope, jumped across a sodden slip of ground, and dropped our equipment next to the furrowed trunk of an old cottonwood.

After the fusion of sweat and shade had cooled our skin, Terry suggested that we first use the dip nets to capture tadpoles and insects. I volunteered to wade in barefoot, but stepping into the muck seemed wrong somehow, a violation. My sucking footsteps disturbed a Mexican garter snake, which Terry caught and immediately dropped when he noticed the snake's defensive odor. I chased down and trapped a half-dozen aquatic beetles, water boatmen, and dragonfly larvae with the assistance of densely woven algae barriers. I couldn't find any tadpoles—but the monsoon season hadn't started yet. If Terry wanted tadpoles for his pond, he'd have to return in a couple of weeks without me.

When a huge dark shape suddenly darted out of the blackness, I jumped back but managed to net it anyway. Its size, nearly two and a half inches, and triangular wing pattern looked familiar. It was a giant water bug, a carnivorous insect with piercing mouth parts and a nasty reputation for drilling holes into the toes of waders. Terry wanted to keep one for his aquarium, and I soon captured an even more provocative specimen—a male with rows of clear eggs cemented to its back, where its mate had recently laid them. The males of this animal can't escape the burden of rearing their young.

Sitting at the edge of the water, I rinsed the black pelt of mud from my legs and watched as Terry pulled up cattails for a green border around his camp pond. Mud smeared his thin, white legs where his over-stretched socks had retreated. The picture is as clear to me now as it ever was, and there's a certain poignancy whenever I recall this scene. The missed opportunities. As our friendship eroded over the years after I went to prison, I would return to this place often, in my mind, in my writing. The composer Ned Rorem says that friendship isn't about duration but intensity, and in this case I want to agree with him. I want to believe that despite what I would do to our relationship in the end, despite the regrets I feel today, we had been friends.

That afternoon, we left Twin Ponds to the zigzagging patrols of dragonflies, never to return there again together. A lone thunderhead swelled above the Catalinas, but it was only a false pregnancy. In the heat, seeds baked underground, waiting for rain.

first time

You feel so empty you can't even cry.

The crack of the judge's gavel resounds in your ears as a punctuation mark on your life while two guards half-carry you through a doorway, remove your shackles, and leave you in a steel-walled holding tank. The vomit and urine smell like guilt, at the same time both bitter and deserved. A small window opens and disembodied hands receive your identity—watch, wallet, two quarters and a dime, keys. A voice orders you to strip when a bright orange jumpsuit appears. Plastic slippers replace your oxfords. All you possess goes into a brown paper bag. Then you wait. On one of the yellow walls someone has scratched a desperate petition: "Dear God, where are you when I need you?" Below it, God answers in thin penciled lines: "You did the crime, now do the time."

You measure time in exaggerated degrees, a steady seepage of reality, tiny grains of sanity slipping between numb fingers to be carried off by

---

Above: Arizona State Prison

roaches. Colorless blotches march up your arms, and like the enclosing walls, your flesh grows chalky and cold. You think your skin might become a loose-fitting carapace that once held someone with thoughts and emotions, but no longer. As you've become separated from society, so you've become detached from your humanity. Outcast. Caring about anything causes pain. You know you're in the right place. The empty cell embodies who you are.

You wait on the floor of the tank, your mind locked onto the events of your crime. You've awakened from a dream and nothing has changed. *How could I have done this?* You berate yourself. *What possesses me?* There's a familiarity within you, a feral presence, and you despise it. It clings to you with spider's legs. If you could scrape it off you might, but it's part of you, a comfortable darkness.

Expectation rises with the sound of keys. When the heavy door opens, a huge woman in a brown uniform enters and orders you against the wall. She replaces the chains. The thin flesh around your ankles and wrists chaffs where metal clamps against bone. "Let's go," she says in monotone. "You're going to protective custody." She walks behind you, taking short steps to match your own. The chain between your legs whips back and forth across the concrete as you struggle with the unnatural gait. At the end of the corridor another over-fleshed, androgynous guard rattles a large key in the lock, pulls on the door, and waits. Inside the dim cell a single steel cot holds a plastic mattress without sheets or blankets. The guard fumbles with the locks on your restraints and pulls them away. The door clangs shut and you are left alone again. You like being alone.

Hours pass. In the silence, you think about the former occupant of your cell, who only yesterday committed suicide with a stolen or overlooked razor. Protective custody was his opportunity to escape. A black stain in the center of the floor draws your eyes and holds them.

Again the guards come and replace the shackles. Forcing you out of your security hole, they take you deeper inside the county jail. Somewhere a faceless administrator has begun directing your life, shuttling you around on a whim. Fear ripens as you realize they are taking you to join the inmate population. Recently you've learned that inmates make distinctions concerning crimes. Some, like murder and assault, are acceptable. Yours is not. But showing fear is weakness and nearly as dangerous as a sex crime. Survival means eliminating emotion—and learning other kinds of lies.

Endless, unwashed corridors unwind in the yellow light. You feel the walls more than see them. Their weight grows heavy in your mind with each step. The outside world recedes into an abstraction. There's no possible way out. And then the sound of your footfalls gives way to other sounds, distant shouts and a metallic drumming. Behind these walls are men in cages. The rattle of keys is a signal for many of them to register their complaints and requests, shouting through a narrow slot in the door. The guards ignore their narrow faces, unlocking your shackles and the door and pushing you inside.

The door closes with a sound that could splinter fresh bones. You look around the pod for an empty bed but there isn't one. Eyes stare back at you as you walk down a barred aisle and peer into each cell. Men are everywhere. Their faces are Hispanic, Native American, Black, and Anglo, all of them drawn and unshaven. They wear orange suits like yours, only dingy and wrinkled. Some don't have shoes. In the last cell at the end of the aisle you find a cracked, plastic-coated mattress on the floor, and here you carve out your territory.

One day oozes into another: sleep interrupted by tasteless meals called, appropriately, "chow." Breakfast is at six every morning, but morning is a relative term, something that comes after a time of loud card games and snoring and yellow lights dimmed for sleeping. It's never dark. Paint coats the barred windows, sealing out any natural light. You know they serve breakfast at sunrise only because at this time a solitary cactus wren habitually ratchets its voice beyond the layers of bars, torn wire mesh, and opaque glass. The bird calls you to remember freedom, which seems both inches away . . . and years. When the doors to the cages open remotely, everyone leaves his cell. This is an order, although you've never heard a guard give it. Forty men herd themselves into two dayrooms whose doors close automatically. You wait without words for trays of cold food to appear through the slot in the door, fighting a grogginess that comes from too much sleep and too little activity.

You can't recall your appetite. The breakfast turns your stomach. The leathery eggs without recognizable yolks smell like grease scraped from a stovetop. The butterless toast is limp; the potatoes look green. You give your food to someone who doesn't care about its taste and gulp down your thin coffee. It has a metallic bite as though filtered through steel wool. While everyone eats, the guards appear to count each man and inspect the cells. They circle around you outside the bars, walking the perimeter along a narrow space that separates the inner pod from the outer block walls. From there, they might safely hose you down if necessary. You wait for the men to finish eating so you can go back to sleep and ease the gnawing depression. Some of the men receive a daily issue of psychoactive drugs, freely prescribed by the resident psychiatrist. You could get a dosage too, just by asking, but you don't, preferring to do your time hard. You drop back onto your mattress and stare at the dirty yellow ceiling until most of the pod is asleep, at which time you use the toilet and shower. This affords you the greatest amount of privacy, since the pair of stainless steel commodes lacks stalls and the shower a curtain. At mid-morning the men begin to stir. Another card game is attracting players and spectators in one of the dayrooms. On the floor in an adjacent cell, two men study a chess board. They've expertly molded the pieces—rooks, knights, pawns, each in fine detail—from a putty of toilet paper and toothpaste. One of your cell mates keeps watch for the guards while an artist works on the back of his shoulder. Ink mixed from cigarette ash and saliva, and a staple attached to the handle of a toothbrush, make a jailhouse tattoo. The name of a lover slowly appears each time the artist wipes away the blood. You agree that immortalizing her in this way will keep her from straying, and you want one too.

One of last night's new admissions to the pod is an alcoholic. He hasn't moved from the floor and his vomit. An overweight Native American huddles in the corner of one cell, drooling on himself and muttering. He was arrested for trespassing after breaking into a warehouse only three days after getting out of prison. The police found him inhaling paint from a paper sack. A young Mexican national, transferred from "the Walls" at the Florence state prison, waits trial on new charges. "Street charges," he says in a heavy accent as if boasting, for stabbing a rival gang member. The teardrop tattoo in the corner of one eye, his badge of honor for the murder, is still fresh. He has served seven years already and now will probably get a life sentence.

For lunch, they pass out bologna on plain white bread and barley soup. The soup is watery; the bread sticks to the roof of your mouth with each wooden bite, but loosens with a swallow of cherry Kool-Aid. Eating is an unconscious ritual. Food seems unimportant. It sustains a body that loses weight regardless, but you don't care. Those around you feel differently, however, and are quick to help themselves to any uneaten portion that you leave alone for more than a few seconds. Jailhouse rules: food that sits is anyone's.

You pass the afternoon stretched out on a woolen blanket you've finally been issued, reading a Louis L'Amour western. The only other choices for escape are crime novels. When a guard places a phone in one of the dayrooms, you wait your turn to call your wife and hope that she will be home, that she will accept the charges. She, most of all, has been devastated by your crime, and will continue to be, regardless of whether she decides to salvage the marriage. Your two baby girls are too young to understand what's happening, except that daddy won't be coming home for a long time. Your unborn child may never even know you until she's in her teens.

The walls and bars and men disappear with the sound of her voice. "I miss you," she says, and you begin to cry. *She's in prison, too,* you think. *Her crime is loving me.* You sob then, losing control, hoping that no one will notice. She holds you with her words; you see your tears falling on her breasts—and then your time is up. Before you can tell her that you love her, reality returns with the sound of a dial tone. Disoriented, you stumble back to your bunk and discover that someone has stolen your blanket.

Dinner is a repeat of lunch and breakfast; only the shape of the food changes. A dead insect stares at you from under the chicken fried steak.

You're learning to sleep with the light and noise. You lie on one side until you're uncomfortable, then roll over on your back, then to your other side. Without any sheets, your mattress feels like a plastic-coated, swamp cooler pad and adheres to your skin. Finally, you draw your knees to your chest, cradle your head in your hands, and wait. The ventilation system creates a draft that doesn't remove the stale air but only pushes it around. The tobacco fog above your head is omnipresent, fed by tendrils of smoke that curl away from all of the bunks. Everyone smokes but you, and you consider starting. Trash, cigarette butts and ash, and gobs of mucus carpet the perimeter aisle, but your stomach no longer heaves at the sight of it. The men find the walkway a convenient toilet, and it must be hosed down every morning. You go back to your book. At eleven o'clock everyone is locked into his cell, but the noise still doesn't quit—conversations, yelling, banging, laughter—it won't get quiet until after breakfast.

The cycle never changes. It carries on from sleeping to eating to sleeping to restless periods of inactivity until more and more empty days simply pass. Stale tobacco and unwashed bodies no longer defile your senses. The odor saturates your clothing, your hair. You're becoming desensitized to the smell of desperate men.

Then one day they ship you from the county jail to the Department of Corrections and the state prison system. A county sheriff shackles you and drives you to a reception and treatment center in Phoenix known as Alhambra. You're nervous. Things concerning you are happening, but you're told nothing except "roll up." At Alhambra, officers add you to a homogeneous group of inmates, all dressed in orange jumpsuits and slippers. The brick building could be a college dormitory. Four wings, enclosing an inner courtyard, hold hundreds of inmates waiting processing and classification before being assigned to one of the prison yards scattered around the state. Inside, wide hallways with freshly waxed floors lead to hundreds of cells. In one of these a guard points to a mattress on the floor. "That's yours," he says. There are four other men in the two-man cell.

Meals at Alhambra taste better than county jail. Instead of being bland

and cold, they are only bland. You realize that a paper napkin is a luxury. After every meal a line forms at the chow hall exit where the guards frisk you, patting down back and chest, legs and groin in search of stolen utensils. The women officers are especially thorough with their hands.

The classification committee wants to know why you didn't run while out on bond before your sentencing. You can't answer them because you don't know. They want you to sign a waiver, releasing the department from responsibility for your safety. If you refuse, you'll spend the next twelve years in protective custody. Hard time.

"Don't tell anyone what you're in for," one of the men advises. "You'll need to make up a story and stick to it."

"Keep to yourself," another says. "When you have to fight, make a lot of noise. That'll bring the guards."

You leave the committee feeling confused and anxious about what awaits you in prison. It's foreign to you; you've never lived on the streets or associated with gangs. Your college education and teaching career hasn't prepared you for this subculture. When an officer locks you in your cell for the remainder of the night a sense of security replaces your anxiety. You're liking confinement more and more.

At three o'clock in the dark of one morning you're woken, led to a room with buzzing fluorescent lights, and strip-searched. You and thirty other men are being transferred. You hand over your jumpsuits, shoes, and underwear and stand naked in a circle while uniformed men scrutinize the orifices of your bodies. "Feet apart," an officer commands, "bend over and spread 'em." Without dignity, there's no embarrassment; without pride, there's no shame. You do as you are told, like an animal lacking spirit or will. After you dress, they give you a number—61728—and tell you to memorize it. It's another unfelt humiliation; you no longer have a name. Then the officers chain you all together and load you into an ancient school bus modified with steel mesh window screens and bound for the state penitentiary.

The bus ride is hot and dirty. Your legs cramp from sitting in a seat designed for grade school children. You ignore it, concentrating on what you can see through the window webbing. You've driven this stretch of highway for years, but you've never really seen it until now. You want to memorize every tree and rock, every signpost and billboard. You consider what every person you see is thinking, wondering what they're all doing, where they are going, and you wish you could be any one of them. Along the highway leading to the prison, power poles stand erect like wooden crosses lining the road to Rome.

The administration building at the Santa Rita Unit hides the ugliness that exists beyond its electronic doors. With flags waving, it looks like the visitor center of a national park. Inmate workers in blue uniforms maintain the landscaping. Trees shade park benches and a perfectly manicured Bermuda lawn. But where you're going, a twelve-foot maze of steel mesh, capped with spirals of razor wire, encloses a twenty-acre compound—the "yard." Four housing units, block structures of ninety-six double-bunked cells, house about 750 medium security inmates. Patches of grass and a few skeletal trees relieve some of the barrenness of gray and open space. Beyond the fences and prison walls, a range of mountains—the Santa Ritas—lifts up another ragged barrier, but this one is welcome. It allows your eyes a place to rest.

You change into your prison-issue, Brander's blue jeans and chambray shirt, and an officer escorts you to your cell. "If you have any problems with your cell mate," she tells you, "let me know. He's at work now."

You remain silent and she leaves. Your cell is a seven-by-twelve concrete box. Its two beds, metal shelves and desk, toilet and sink fill most of the space. Among the cardboard property boxes, books, and clothing, there's little room to move around, except on your bunk. You think you're living in a bathroom, but it feels secure.

Later, during recreation time, you venture out of your cell. You're acutely aware that your ill-fitting and stiff clothing marks you as a new arrival, but what you can't see is the expression on your face that says "fish." You avoid eye contact, keep your distance and stare at the ground when anyone comes near you. You're fearful of unknowingly breaching the convict code, a set of unwritten rules brutally enforced by the inmates who control the yard. You're playing the game without understanding all the rules. You know about snitching and mixing with other races. You'd rather not find out about other rules the hard way.

Gatherings of men, each group bound together by similar color, form along the runs, at tables, in the laundry room. Some play cards or slap dominoes, others talk quietly among themselves. You notice eyes watching you. Men drag rakes in the pea gravel or sweep the endless concrete walkways and courts or scrub shower stalls. Others lift iron at the weight pile or walk counterclockwise along the half-mile exercise track. Mexican nationals chase a soccer ball in the center field of the circular track; teams of black men shoot basketballs at netless hoops, shirts versus skins. The small education classes have many empty chairs. You ask one of the teachers about an opening for a teacher's aide and she gives you an application. It's one of the best jobs on the yard and pays up to fifty cents an hour after a short two years. You neglect to tell her that you've taught in public school. It's too close to your crime.

As weeks blend into months, keeping to yourself becomes increasingly difficult. Your job in education forces you to mix with other inmates. You could make your students pay for extra help, like the barber who charges packs of cigarettes for a better haircut or the food service workers who charge sodas for larger portions, but you don't. Getting caught trading and bartering means a disciplinary write-up, which could mean a loss of visits with family or a transfer to higher custody. It's bad enough dealing with all the petty rules: keeping your mustache trimmed to military regulation, shaving daily, tucking in your shirt, making your bed, staying off the grass, not loitering in the administration area. You don't need to add to your insecurities by getting in trouble with the guards.

Debts and bartering seem a way of life here. Food is stolen from the chow halls and resold. Some inmates run stores, stocking popular commissary items like candy bars and snack cakes and reselling them at twice the cost. Two for one, they call it. This gives those without money on their inmate accounts an opportunity to go into debt, running up bills until the debtor ends up in protective isolation. Gambling and drugs also create debts. You've seen more illegal drugs in prison than in your previous "free" life. The department tells the public that all drugs come through visitation. But you know who on the staff to go to for cocaine, heroin, speed, marijuana—all available, for a price. The men brew home-made hooch from fruit, juice, even chocolate chip cookies. Others sell sexual favors. Young men, those under twenty in prison for the first time, may become sex slaves for older men, who provide for and protect them in return. Few consider themselves homosexual; they say they're just in prison. You sympathize with all the men with uncontrollable habits, the deviants and abusers, the abused. There's no possibility of receiving help in this place.

After several empty years have passed, you feel acclimated to the prison culture but never completely secure. You worry about the one wrong word or move that will bring your whole world down on you, ending your job, cell assignment, yard assignment—every mote of control you've gained. In this environment, they could ship you to another facility in a corner of the state too far for your family to travel for weekend visits. Or you could earn a "jacket" (like snitch) that puts your life in jeopardy on any yard and spend your remaining years without seeing the sky. That none of this has happened, even for years, doesn't make you fear it any less. Fear is a presence, always. It's like living with an undiscovered tumor. Sometimes you catch yourself wishing, under all this mind-bending sameness, that the end would just happen.

Your friends are people you previously would never have spoken to; you fight being like them, thinking like them, talking like them. The culture both repulses and attracts you with its childish self-centeredness, arrogance, and stupidity. Many inmates have a strength of heart but no conscience; the state has raised them in the juvenile system and graduated them to adult prison. They are reckless and dangerous because they don't value life.

At thirty-two years of age you feel old. Your body is adjusting to a sedentary existence. Lines crease your face. An inmate barber has pointed out your receding hairline. White hair populates the parts of your head you can't reach with tweezers. Although you walk laps like a dog in a kennel, wearing a path just inside the perimeter fence, the starch-laden food only adds flesh to your waist. The prison dentist wants to pull a few teeth, his solution for aggressive cavities.

With your physical atrophy come the emotional problems. Feelings of helplessness and loss, of a world passing you by, press on you. Previous relationships crumble with the lack of real attention. Friends drift away, their letters—what convicts call "love"—no longer arrive. Mail call causes emotional swings from hope to depression every day except Sundays and holidays. Your family visits less often—they hate this place and you can't blame them. Visiting your wife erases your fences but raises hers. When you're with her you understand what it means to be touch-deprived. Her eyes look past you; her kiss is perfunctory. She says she wants to keep the marriage together, but the pain of watching you disintegrate in prison, the humiliation of welfare and food stamps, the difficulty of raising your children alone, only adds to the gravity of her own sexual frustration. You fear she may find escape and relief in the arms of another man. You've seen it happen in prison. One day you're paged for legal mail and an officer serves you divorce papers without warning or explanation. You call home and she's changed her number. The last seed of your hope has proven infertile; it dies as you discover you have no choice but to sign away the remnants of a former life. These thoughts are always with you; you can't shake them even in your sleep. You're alone in the pain of it, afraid to speak about it. If it happens, you hope you can win her back, and if not, that you will at least see your children again.

More years pass. When you need surgery for infected tonsils, two armed guards handcuff and shackle your arms to your waist and drive you to a local hospital. You wear an oversized jumpsuit of biohazard orange. Shuffling to the ward under escort, you keep your eyes unfocused, your face expressionless. People stare at you, and you feel a kind of pride that comes with being feared and despised. The guards chain you to a hospital bed and shadow you. Nurses prepare you for surgery with words directed only at the officers. "Can you remove the handcuffs?" one of them asks. "No, Ma'am. We can't do that," a guard answers. You say nothing. The carapace that originally offered protection has thickened and hardened with time, with each affront to your humanity. You are an emotional desert.

Society calls you hopeless, and you accept it. You're anxious in an uncontrolled world. You don't know how to act around free people. You believe they see you as hard and cold, like the chains that hold you. They make you conscious of your crime, rubbing it in your face. *He's sick,* they all think. *He deserves what he got . . . more than he got.* Prison, you realize, protects you from society. It's the only place you feel normal.

When you return, the electric motor groans and the steel doors slam behind you. The punctuation rings in your ears, but the sound comforts you. Halfway across the yard your former anxiety dissipates. You're aware that it smells different here—that same desperate stink—but that too is welcome. It lingers in your nostrils for a few minutes and then fades. You don't hear the shouts of men or see the fences crowned with coils of razor wire. The structures and sensual violations of prison have become your domain.

You are home.

campo bonito

A rust-eaten, forest service sign warned us about impending travel conditions: Primitive Road Hazardous to Public Use. *What road?* I thought, glancing at my wife who'd gone rigid, gripping her seat and reproaching me with her eyes. I proceeded anyway, splashing through an algae-curdled streamlet and attempting to straddle a deeply rutted track that climbed through a barrier of manzanita before opening into a clearing. After a nine-year absence, we had come back to Campo Bonito.

I parked near a crumbling stone chimney. Karen and I stepped from the security of our car, followed by our three daughters, Jessica, now twelve, ten-year-old Kasondra, and eight-year-old Melissa. Immediately we felt it—like something was watching us. A Presence seemed to permeate the place. I recognized it as in previous years, attributing the feeling to the history of Campo Bonito, to voices calling out of the past from every empty foundation. All around us, cracked and weathered cement

---

Above: Ruin at Campo Bonito

slabs fought nature's persistent reclamation; a few had already surrendered to the scrub vegetation and rocky soil. Only irises, feral descendants of flowers once tended by miners' wives, revealed the outlines of buried cabin floors. For many decades they'd unfurled their purple and white blossoms for no one but deer and javelina. Even the giant black walnut trees, which previously had offered children a cool place to play, now wasted their shade on cattle.

Except for the foundation terraces and strange ambiance, you wouldn't know that at the beginning of the twentieth century, Campo Bonito had boomed as one of several mining communities surrounding Oracle, Arizona. In its heyday, more than three hundred men worked the claims under nearby Apache Peak, their families living in the mining camp. Along with its ore processing equipment—a locomotive-type boiler, stamping mill, and narrow-gauge railroad—Campo Bonito had a large common mess hall, a well, and many crude buildings that served its residents. Campo Bonito got its name from a hopeful chicken farmer from Denver, Colorado. The story goes that a certain Dr. Scudder left his wife and family in Denver, found this place, and began constructing their future out of thousands of adobe bricks: a chicken ranch. Borrowing a Spanish dictionary from his closest neighbors, William and Elizabeth Wood, he chose the words *Campo Bonito,* an appropriate name for what he considered his "beautiful camp." But Dr. Scudder's dream would never produce a single egg. Soon after his disapproving young wife arrived (trailing velvet, it is said), the doctor's plans turned infertile and he returned to Denver. The name, however, stuck.

One central figure was responsible for much of the mining activity at Campo Bonito: a flamboyant western circus star named Colonel William F. "Buffalo Bill" Cody. Unfortunately, his whole operation, which cost hundreds of thousands of dollars in the end, would prove fruitless. In the last years of his life, William Cody would squander his wealth and retirement, duped into believing the exaggerated tales of gold in the northern foothills of the Santa Catalina Mountains.

Late afternoon sunlight slanted through three huge walnut trees at the upper end of the clearing, adding visual texture to the already palpable atmosphere. Other trees—hackberry, oak, and sycamore—outlined an arroyo that bordered us on the south. The length of the clearing's northern flank comprised a low, grassy hill, spotted with juniper and manzanita. This arrangement, enclosed by hills and ridges and peaks, made my daughters wonder if we wouldn't find elves hunting in the surrounding woodland.

High winter rainfall in the area had resulted in heavy spring growth. Perennial grasses, now bleaching to straw as the foresummer drought approached, furred the hills. Wildflowers like globemallow, fleabane, and thistle contributed their shades of orange and blue and lavender, respectively. An abandoned peach tree was heavy with hard, green leaves. Karen selected a spot of level ground near the peach tree for our picnic, food being her first order of business. I finished unloading the car, setting out tarps and ice chests under the canopy of the closest walnut.

It was at this exact spot, sixteen years previous, that I first camped with Karen only days after we had met at the nearby YMCA camp. Her kiss and our subsequent romance were still two weeks away, hardly an unhatched dream in my mind, but I remember my attraction to her. The entire camp staff had finished dinner—shish kebabs and Dutch oven pineapple upside-down cake—and we had rekindled the fire to drive off the mosquitoes, which even then, I'm sure, attacked me but ignored Karen. The evening enhanced every sound: the snapping of burning branches, the call of a Mexican jay, footsteps, our voices—normally insignificant noises until darkness. A hemisphere of campfire light illuminated the oaks and walnuts. As the trees on our perimeter began to shift and dance, above us branches of light and shadow writhed together like courting snakes.

Karen had retreated from the group to her tube tent, a simple construction of bright orange fabric rolled into a cylinder and staked at the far end. Inside, her candle flickered as she wrote in her journal. A night wind was rising, moaning through the trees and canyons as if frustrated by the encounters. With every mercurial gust her tent took a breath, inflating its nylon lung to capacity in a quiet pop. I recognized her as different from most of us, and not because she was the only person who had brought her own tent. She was quiet, rather than overly social, yet she seemed confident without having to prove herself in any way. When I stopped by her tent that night out of curiosity, I left wanting to get to know her more.

Over the years, Karen and I would return dozens of times to Campo Bonito. Few places were as absolute as those moonless nights there. Away from the light of our campfire, the stars seemed at arm's length. Always, I would search among them for two constellations, Scorpio and Cassiopeia, which in those northern foothills of the Catalinas where the night sky was free of incandescence, shone with a brilliance that only unadulterated eyes could see.

But even under the skies of the Tucson prison complex, I could find those constellations, the weight of their witness pressing on me. The pair will always hold a certain poignancy for me as they usher in the summer season. When the YMCA camp opened for my last summer, I walked its trails at night, Scorpio and Cassiopeia rising high like my emotions.

After our picnic lunch, my family and I hiked south to the Pure Gold and Maudina tungsten mines, first opened in the 1880s but now played out for many years. The old mining road, so severely eroded that it served more as a ditch for runoff, narrowed as it climbed and then began tracing the contours of the hills. Vegetation encroached. High above Campo Bonito we could see where the foothills of the Catalinas relaxed into the wide San Pedro Valley, which in turn, faded into a distant range of gray mountains: the Galiuros. What caught my attention, however, wasn't the distant landscape. For the first time since that summer of 1986, more than nine years before, my eyes rested on the YMCA camp. Farthest from the camp's center, Unit Five's cabins, where I first counseled older boys, studded the highest hill. Below these, other buildings spread across the folded desert grassland: the rectangular dining hall and blue swimming pool, the horse corrals and water tanks, Terry Hutchin's nature center, and the outdoor chapel where Karen and I were married. I knew the place as home—its every tree and stone, the musty smell of its decades-old structures, its stories—but I could never return there. For Karen, there were ghosts walking around camp that she dared not encounter. And I had a few of my own.

The old mining road disappeared altogether where a valley formed a narrow V high on the mountainside. We counted a dozen holes, like the nests of giant cicada-killing wasps, behind broken rocks that had trundled down the hillsides. Massive timbers, the supporting skeleton of a decomposing ore chute, protruded from one of the largest tailings. Refuse was everywhere—bent sheets of corrugated metal, split pipes and twisted rails, hundreds of crushed tin cans—rusting in the rubble of what appeared to be the aftermath of a landslide.

Dean Prichard, present owner of Buffalo Bill's cabin and High Jinks mine, once told me that he'd explored a couple dozen or more of these mines. They must riddle the whole mountain. I'd spoken with him on several occasions about Campo Bonito's history. In his courtyard at nearby High Jinks Ranch, the remains of a Packard touring car—like the one William Cody drove to Campo Bonito in 1911—rusted in a bed of irises. Maybe it *was* Buffalo Bill's. Dean also told me he'd found a Spanish sword near the mines, motivation enough for me to poke around a bit.

Karen and the girls waited in the sun while I explored one of the tunnels. The smell of mildew rising on a cool draft confronted me at the entrance. Somewhere in the mine's recesses water dripped into a pool, but the cloudy beam of my flashlight failed to locate the source of the sound. Rock walls enclosed me, walls unsupported by timbers, which made me nervous. The tunnel appeared solid, however, as though it were carved through bedrock. Where the shaft angled left fifty yards into the mountain, probably following the course of a mineral vein, water flooded its floor and I had to turn back. No bats or black-tailed rattlesnakes that time, only spindly-legged spiders.

I wanted to repeat history and climb over the saddle above the tungsten mines into Southern Belle Canyon, but Karen and the girls were resistant. I had told them the story and that was enough: Around 1880, a young woman from Virginia found gold on the other side of the ridge after she literally sat down on it. Her name was Gillette Young, wife of Captain John T. Young, and she used to bake pies and carry them in a tin bucket to her husband working a claim under Apache Peak that he called the Imperial Mine. One day, after crossing this saddle, Gillette stopped to rest on an outcrop of rock under some oak trees. Without thinking about it, she began picking at a whitish vein with her hairpin when she noticed a dull yellow color. She quickly gathered some pieces in her handkerchief and brought them to her husband at the Imperial. They both rushed back to the sight, where John Young pried off some larger specimens from the blanket ledge and exclaimed that it was the richest ore he had ever seen. Forgetting about Gillette's lunch, the two spent the rest of the day constructing a discovery monument and stepping off and marking a twenty-acre claim.

John Young named the claim for his wife: Southern Belle.

During our first summers at the camp, when Karen and I worked as counselors, I often hiked with the oldest boys past these mines to the Outpost in Southern Belle Canyon. Occasional animal trails relieved us of bushwhacking up the steep incline, where sheets of leaf litter made progress slow and slippery. The oaks and juniper thinned as we approached the crest of the saddle, which freed us from the closeness of the woodland and allowed rising air currents to cool our flushed skin.

We slipped, slid, hopped, and bounced down into the valley, carefully avoiding the prickly pear and agave. Near the Southern Belle tunnels, loose tailings like earth-flows provided routes of quick descent, although my boots sank easily into the soft scree. Where the oaks returned on the canyon floor, amber water pulsed over white granite boulders and spilled into shallow pools. Fleets of water striders rippled their surfaces while braces of sulphur butterflies orbited clumps of orange globemallow.

A rough jeep track paralleled the stream and led us farther up the canyon. Along its margins, thistles and prickly poppies and more globemallows bloomed where squawbush and silktassel gave way to open, rocky ground. Then, on the right side of the road beneath several large oaks, a stone wall and three terraces appeared—all that remained of

Charley Brajevich's cabin, and what we called the Outpost. The wall, a masonry construction that was still in fair condition, stood eight feet high against an encroaching hill. Behind it, a short distance uphill, the shell of a water tank sat partially crushed, rusting, half-buried. A section of pipe drifted in the direction of a well.

Serious mining began in this canyon after 1879 when two prospectors, B. N. "Charley" Brajevich and John Ivancovich, found a 6 1/3-ounce gold nugget under Apache Peak. As news of gold circulated around the Oracle mining camp, more prospectors came and staked their claims. And then Gillette Young stumbled upon the Southern Belle. In no time, New Yorker James W. "Ed" Fellowes offered to buy the claim from the Youngs for fifteen hundred dollars. Because the two were in financial trouble, they took the money. Ed Fellowes then set up a ten-stamp mill near the mine, using a team of twenty-four mules to drag a heavy boiler up the canyon. Over the next three years, he mined eighteen thousand tons of gold ore, a boom that attracted more prospectors until miners held the entire region in a checkerboard pattern of claims. At the mouth of Southern Belle Canyon, a small settlement sprang up, complete with crude camp buildings, a general store, and a saloon and dance hall. Although the boom shortly turned to bust, when Southern Belle closed around 1885, it had produced half a million dollars in gold.

After 1885, the Southern Belle went through periods of dormancy, light work by a relative of Fellowes, and subleasing by mine promoters. But as activity at the Southern Belle subsided, other mines attracted players, among them the Morning Star and Maudina tungsten, which created the settlement at Campo Bonito. Around 1902, William Cody started investing in the mines at Campo Bonito. It is unknown what originally spurred his interest. One story relates Cody's fascination with the legendary "Mine with the Iron Door," a seventeenth century Jesuit treasure supposedly lost somewhere near Oracle. Another claims influence by Captain John D. Burgess, a former army scout and old friend of Cody's. Burgess had been prospecting and promoting mines in southern Arizona for many years, but without much commercial success (although he was good at raising money). At Campo Bonito, he owned a few claims and had built a stamping mill with another investor who later ended the partnership after sinking five thousand dollars into an unproductive venture. Burgess needed new investors. Cody was wealthy and looking to retire. And so Burgess persuaded Cody to take a partnership, together with a New York mining engineer named L. W. Getchell, in the Campo Bonito Mining and Milling Company. Most of the money, however, came from Buffalo Bill.

For much of that first decade, the Campo Bonito Mining and Milling Company, with Cody as president, continued to buy claims and attract investors, mostly Cody's friends. Although the mines produced some scheelite, a high-grade tungsten ore, they yielded no gold. Assurances of rich veins at the bottom of the next shaft were rife; dividends, nevertheless, were lacking. Cody, believing the fantastic reports of gold and always optimistic about his mines, met every request for more capital. Near the end of the decade, Cody convinced a wealthy friend, former Indian Agent Colonel Daniel B. Dyer, to invest in the Bonito mines. Together they formed the Cody-Dyer Arizona Mining and Milling Company and promptly began buying more claims. One of these was the Southern Belle. A mine promoter from San Francisco named McIsaacs had made a good run with the mine and then skipped out with the proceeds, leaving his bills unpaid. The Cody-Dyer company put up seventy thousand dollars for property payments and some development, securing the Southern Belle under bond and lease.

Buffalo Bill Cody didn't visit his mines until the spring of 1911 when he came to Oracle in his Packard touring car. He stayed at the then-famous Mountain View Hotel (now a Baptist church), which was owned by a friend from his scouting days, William Neal. Elizabeth Lambert Wood, a resident of Oracle and soon-to-be friend of Cody's wife, Louisa (Lulu), would later write: "The few people—perhaps thirty-five—then residing in Oracle, gathered to meet him. The instant the Colonel saw William Neal, he called, 'Hello there, Curly. How are you?'" According to Mrs. Wood, Cody then examined a scar across the top of Neal's head, a bullet groove from their Indian campaign days. Both laughed upon recalling the incident.

Within a year of his arrival, Cody had grown suspicious of his mine promoters. Louisa Cody, who was neither interested in her husband's show business career nor his mining ventures, probably suggested that something was amiss. Colonel Dyer must have had his doubts too. Since he knew nothing of the business, Dyer sent for his nephew, an Idaho mining engineer named E. J. Ewing who arrived incognito in February, 1912, to report on the operation. Within a few days he had uncovered a scheme to separate Cody and Dyer from as much of their money as possible. In his words, "The management was engaged in dubious practices."

Ewing's first indication of a scam came as he watched a miner slowly adding high-grade tungsten ore from a sack into the feed stream of a crusher, effectively "salting" the machine to make ore samples from certain mines appear richer in minerals. This would inflate the value of a claim that promoters could then sell to the partners at huge profits. Ewing also discovered, along with fabulous reports of gold and ghost payrolls, that Nobel Getchell, the son of L. W. Getchell, was taking kickbacks for selling worthless claims to the company. (Ewing could never prove Getchell senior's involvement with any misdealing.) After Ewing approached Cody with the evidence, the circus star threatened the Getchells with arrest and prosecution, at which point the two turned over their stock and some money. Cody never followed through with any legal action, probably because of the adverse publicity it would bring him.

To deal with the fiasco, Ewing took charge, firing miners, reorganizing, and advising the partners to close the Southern Belle, Morning Star, and Maudina mines and scale down their other operations. It wasn't until the fall of 1915 that Ewing decided the price of tungsten would make limited mining profitable, but by then neither Cody nor Dyer, who were both very sick, could make a move. In the end, the partners owned nearly two hundred worked-out properties that had little or no resale value. There's a story that one of Cody's most prized possessions did come out of his mines—not gold or silver or tungsten but a jaguar—a rare visitor to the Southwest even then. One of his Mexican workers trapped and killed the large cat, thinking it was a mountain lion. He gave its skin to Cody as a gift.

In 1916, Cody spent his last winter at Campo Bonito. He died on January 10 of the following year and was buried at Lookout Mountain, Colorado.

Although Buffalo Bill's mining endeavors were a failure, his presence at Campo Bonito gained the community much celebrity. From his plush cabin retreat, built over his High Jinks mine (where Dean Prichard now lives), he entertained the families of his mining company and visiting friends. One of his most noteworthy performances involved a role for which his long white hair and beard suited him. On Christmas Day, 1912, families at Campo Bonito had gathered in the mess hall to welcome the arrival of a special guest. At noon, Cody appeared, dressed as Santa Claus and carrying gifts for everyone. He had planned a day of holiday festivities—sporting events for children and their parents—topping it all off with a dance in the evening.

Cody would spend his last years frustrated and discouraged. The popularity of his wild west show had waned, and the business concerning his mines had robbed him of a comfortable retirement. It's anyone's guess whether or not he questioned himself, pouring the last fourteen years of his life into a foolish fantasy and in the end having nothing to show for it. Certainly his wife and friends must have doubted his sanity.

Instead of hiking to Southern Belle Canyon that afternoon, Karen and the girls and I climbed into the hills north of Campo Bonito to search for a grave I once visited as a child. Thick vegetation—thorned and spined, crooked and spindly—surrounded us. Grama grasses crowded among prickly pear, century plants, and sotol. In the wide arroyos and valleys that shaped the hills, vegetation grew impenetrable. Manzanita, squawbush, and silktassel, like green bulwarks, provided cover for cottontail rabbits and Gambel's quail. Karen and I once rode horses to navigate those stands. The extensive fretwork of hard, twisted stems made us wish we were again on horseback.

The girls' lithe frames aided their passage and they soon outpaced me, especially as I kept stopping to scribble notes. Prickly pear cacti, just beginning to bear fat buds, sprawled across the hillsides. Century plants and sotol picketed the skyline with past reproductive efforts, the dried stalks like markers for some nameless miner's test holes. The dead plants drew my attention, and I couldn't help thinking how they suited that place. Yellow, leathery leaves unfurled from the desiccated hearts of the century plants, the leaves still serrated with shark's teeth and tipped like stilettos. Sometime between the age of ten and thirty years (not a hundred as its name suggests), a single flowering stalk will bolt skyward like summer lettuce, growing several inches a day to a height of about twelve feet, placing its reproductive parts well out of reach of browsing deer and cattle. Its stores of energy depleted in branching clusters of yellow flowers and then fruits, the agave, in one shot at the mother lode and immortality, will produce a multitude of seeds and then die.

Sotol, the more graceful of the spent plants, had long, thin, spiny-margined leaves that fanned out from its core in wispy rosettes. It also grows slowly, storing up nutrients until ready to reproduce after fifteen years or so, when it will erupt with nappy, plumelike flower stalks, male and female parts on separate plants. Sotol will bloom for many years; but it, too, eventually depletes its resources and dies, decomposing into the curiously dried leaves called desert spoons.

I kicked one dead, overturned sotol and the tight bowl of its core exploded, scattering individual leaves the size of soup ladles to rattle in the wind. The sight filled me with a sudden sadness. Century plants and sotol took what they could from that place for a dozen or so glorious years and then, like the people once connected to the landscape, left behind their bones.

At the top of a hill, my girls and I stumbled over round, softball-sized rocks, searching among the agave, mesquite, and stiff hummocks of bear-grass for a decades-old image in my mind. Twenty minutes later, Karen found a jumbled and overgrown mound of brown stones that I recognized as the grave.

I first saw it during my week at the YMCA camp when I was twelve years old. We had hiked most of Sunday morning to reach it, sixty boys dressed in T-shirts and jeans, carrying army canteens belted at our hips. Blood pulsing behind our red faces in rhythm to the droning of cicadas seemed to emphasize the midsummer heat. But our camp counselors told us it was imperative that we make the trip. The grave was Pima Joe's, one of Buffalo Bill's Indian miners who'd gotten himself killed in a bitter claim dispute. After the desert gave up his bones, he was buried on that hilltop without ceremony. I remembered that we had to come to the grave as part of our chapel service to take turns at etching the sign of the cross into a stone. According to the legend, Pima Joe's soul wouldn't find rest until we scratched completely through the granite, breaking it in two.

Now, with my wife and daughters beside me, I stared at the grave and thought about the loss. The place was full of the holes of people's dreams, some of them vacant but for spiders, others filled in with rubble and lives. I remembered Charley Brajevich and John Young, William Cody and his miners, and the unnamed women who lifted homes from the dirt and scree and then passed on, leaving behind their flower gardens and fruit trees, planted when hope was brightest. I thought about Elizabeth Wood, who suffered and stayed on the land. And Dean Prichard, another who still remained after a loss. Years ago, his young daughter had ridden her horse into those hills and never rode out again. After the accident, Dean set the horse free, and I've since heard that people occasionally see it on moonlit nights. His pain came close to me that day; I had nearly lost my daughters, too, although the cause for that tragedy rested solely with me.

A shovel handle, furrowed with dry rot but still fashioned into a cross, marked the pile of stones. A tangle of rusted baling wire had lost its grip on the transom and gravity drew the cross askew. The sacrilegious hooves of cattle long ago claimed the oval of wire fence; mashed and twisted, it surrendered to the grass and a bonsai mesquite. The stone cell of Pima Joe's spirit lay partially buried and unbroken, the depression of a cross just discernible on its upper surface. No one came to the grave anymore. The boys at the camp had other adventures that took them not as far.

Crouching at the stone, each of my daughters in turn repeated a ritual long forgotten but now restored. They, at least, believed. When I lifted the fist of quartz to add my own marks to theirs, I included a prayer for one more soul imprisoned by his past failings; this one, for the present, condemned to haunt the old mining community of Campo Bonito.

sleeping with the enemy

My wife is not the enemy. Let's get that straight from the start. And, although our marriage sometimes bruises and blisters both of us (more her than me, I think), I do manage to curl up beside her most nights, even if the only response I get from her is hair in my mouth. So far, Karen has only *suggested*—as a warning should I ever offend her again—that I remove my bedding to the bathtub. She believes the bathroom a more appropriate punishment than the living room couch. Kind of like solitary confinement: a hard bunk with a sink and toilet, a place I'd recently been intimate with for nearly eight years before a judge released me from prison. Karen's warning, like her apparent domineering manner, is more of a pose than a threat. (I hope.) Whatever you may think concerning the following, it isn't sleeping with Karen that plagues me.

I've slept with some strange animals, but I've never slept with a rattlesnake. I've held one as its muscular helix twisted convulsively to under-

---

Above: Kissing bugs *(Triatoma rubida)*

mine my grip and watched its twin hypodermic teeth unfold to shoot oily yellow venom down my arm, but I've never awakened to one curled under my covers. Nor have I felt that quick slap and fiery penetration, that bloating of dying tissue. So far, I've been lucky in my foolishness. I wouldn't mind sleeping with some snakes; the harmless ones don't upset me anymore—bullsnakes with their horseshoe needle tracks at the backs of my knees, kingsnakes hanging from my knuckles, whipsnakes wherever they can reach. It isn't serpents I have a problem sleeping with.

What bothers me are bedmates much more exasperating. What bothers me are bugs. Or, more precisely, arthropods, a group of joint-legged, exoskeletal, exothermic vermin that not only includes bugs but also spiders, scorpions, chiggers, ticks, lice, and mosquitoes. They all get to me. You might say I'm a human bug trap. UV bug zappers, flypaper, roach motels can't attract them like I can. They're *drawn* to me. Amazingly, my wife has found some virtue in this remarkable ability of mine. She says she likes sleeping with me because I persuade all the creeping things that inhabit our desert home to leave her alone. I persuade them to bite, sting, pinch, and suck on me instead. So she rests in perfect comfort, while starving arthropods drain my body by minute degrees for long hours every night during "bug season," which occurs in those months when the thermometer stays above forty. Except for about three days in January, it's always bug season in southern Arizona. I don't mind too much. There are lesser occupations than being her bug repellent.

Blood-sucking bugs. I curse their very existence as the only defect in God's creation. "Blessed be the Lord our God, who introducest variety amongst Thy creatures," says an old Hebrew prayer. I could do with a little less variety. The worst kind are the kissing bugs. These inch-long black parasites with pointed beaks are exquisitely designed for drawing huge quantities of body fluids through tiny holes. The naturalist Richard Jeffries says there's nothing human in nature. I disagree. If I don't consider the insects unnatural, which I'm inclined to do, then there *is* one thing human in nature: my blood *inside* kissing bugs. This year we had a nest of the assassins under our bed. Did they bother Karen? Of course not—not when they had an unlimited reservoir of my precious B positive. On some nights I would wake up with my ears ringing, my scalp and armpits itching, and that body numbness that comes with an allergic reaction to the foreign proteins in bug saliva. With welts rising on my arms or legs, I would strip the bed. But only rarely did I catch the culprit in the act, a frustrating failure because I knew as soon as the lights went out it would be back, driving its lancet mouth parts into my fingers . . . or worse, my lips or eyelids. Even after I broke down our bed and disposed of more than a dozen instars—the flightless juveniles of the bug—they continued to feed on me. Hand picking didn't work. Insecticide had little effect. I even contemplated cocooning myself in mosquito netting. Now I just live with it, consoling myself with the macho idea that I'm protecting Karen by default.

Sometimes I remind her what Carlos Chagas found in Brazil in 1909. He was the first to observe a fatal ailment in humans caused by kissing bugs. Now called Chagas' disease, it affects millions of people every year in tropical America. Kissing bugs transmit the disease by infecting the bite site with a protozoan *(Trypanosoma cruzi)* that the insect usually carries. Symptoms appear in about a week and include fever, anemia, vomiting, and soon enough, if untreated, heart failure. Charles Darwin may have had it, I add, although the disease was unknown in England at his time and his contemporaries thought his complaints were psychosomatic. Darwin wasn't crazy, just beset with pests. Then I tell her about the reports of the parasite living in kissing bugs found in Arizona—no response. But once in a while, I believe I see in her eyes an improved estimation of me. While I root through our sheets, she can sleep, safe from bites, itching, swelling, and fatal diseases.

Karen is always in control. She demonstrates this with ownership—the money, the credit cards, the car—they're all hers. We'll never have signs above a two-car garage that read "Ours" and "Hers." Not because we'll never own two cars, but because, as Karen likes to put it: "What's mine is mine and what's yours is mine." Even the TV remote—I'm ashamed to admit as a member of the male species—is hers. Yet, Karen is my human credential, something that became increasingly clear as the years mounted during my incarceration. She tells me that her issues with control are related to her security, and that feeling secure is more important to her than to me. She's right; all I need to feel secure is a locked door. Karen knows what she wants, and she's not ashamed to take charge of it. She even has control over her own blood supply. No bug dare touch it.

The bug man from Truly Nolen says to get rid of the pack rats. "Kissing bugs live in their nests," he tells me when I complain about them during one of his visits. "No pack rats, no kissing bugs." I find their stick-and-cacti mounds around the house but they are either impenetrable, glued together with their own urine and feces into thorny fortresses, or inaccessible, built within the spiny recesses of a prickly pear cactus. The live trap I borrow works once, and then the rodents begin using it as a feeding station. I consider removing the prickly pear. My final solution, Karen informs me, costs more in maintenance: food, shots, neutering, carpet cleaning. She likes the wildlife—none of it disturbs *her* sleep—and objects to the violence. But I think it will deal naturally with the problem. I get a cat.

So far this year, since Gizmo has discovered the pack rats, I've found one kissing bug in our bed. I keep it in a jar at my desk where I can look at it from time to time. It's dead now. Starvation, I think. Its dried, leg-curled carcass reminds me that some solutions are as easy as getting a cat. And that I can have my own bit of control.

Recently, another kind of nighttime pillager found me in my bed. The bite of this one woke me, and I managed to grab it in the dark. It didn't have the hard carapace of a kissing bug but the soft bulb of a spider. I crushed it and went back to sleep. In the morning a circle of skin on the inside of my upper arm had discolored to black. A hot, red swelling surrounded it from arm pit to elbow. The work of an Arizona brown spider, I thought, the "recluse" of eastern fame.

Brown spiders, like the notorious black widow, have a venomous bite. I knew the details—a blister at the bite sight that ulcerates into a raw, oozing wound that refuses to close. If you're fortunate, you get a nasty scar. Worse cases may lose a limb. I decided to dabble with temptation and experiment with my affliction—it seemed a rare opportunity at the time. I began recording my observations and sensations without seeking medical attention. This went on for a few days before Karen put an end to it and sent me to the health unit at the University of Arizona. As a result, unfortunately, the wound never developed much beyond a white blister centered on a dime of black skin. Interestingly, all of the skin on the palms of my hands and soles of my feet did peel away in great slabs (very grotesque) before the bite finally flaked away as so much dead tissue.

I'll take a brown spider bite anytime over my experiences with several scorpions that have visited me in the night. Two of these encounters happened while camping, reminding me that I have little control over myself no matter where I sleep. The first, the impressively named giant desert hairy, roused me with an introduction on my left ring finger. Thinking I could master the throbbing pain and sleep it off, I laid my head back on my pillow, whereupon the scorpion repeated its call on my earlobe.

When it comes to these arthropods, big doesn't necessarily mean nasty. The venom of the bark scorpion, a small, two-inch species, has killed a few people in Arizona. In Mexico, where the scorpion is more common, about a hundred people die every year. Because the bark scorpion's venom affects the nervous system, other symptoms may accompany a severe burning at the sting site. Once, when I unknowingly welcomed one of these into my warm, comfortable sleeping bag, my guest thanked me by repeatedly thrusting its weaponry into my armpit. Very rude. Aside from the persistent local burn, my hands and feet and face went numb. Then headache and nausea. Muscular weakness in my arms and legs and an inability to focus my eyes followed before recovery several hours later. Steve Prchal, founder of the Sonoran Arthropod Studies Institute in Tucson, has, I think, one of the best descriptions of what the sting feels like: "Take a sharp needle and jab it into your hand. Hold a match or lighter to it for a couple of hours. Then add the needles-and-pins sensation you have when a foot falls asleep."

I've considered getting a bird to deal with the spiders and scorpions—elf owls, I've heard, aside from being inconspicuous in their size and behavior, love scorpions—but I wonder about a bird's compatibility with my cat. Gizmo would just as soon eat a plump owl as a goggle-eyed pack rat. Maybe I'll buy a large lizard, like a green iguana, to help with the house pests . . . and other unwanted guests.

Finally, one other kind of creature has a personal affection for me while ignoring my wife, although she may be sleeping right next to me. They're worse than chiggers, which suffocate under the skin after one or two days with just a few dabs of nail polish. Ticks and lice can be messy, but their threat is mostly in the mind, an innate (primate?) repulsion to crablike bloodsuckers that find a home on our bodies. A little Nix or Quell, some nit-picking, and they're done. No, what eats me at night are the "little flies": mosquitoes.

It seems that since the latest tropical storm abandoned its wet luggage in Tucson, mosquitoes have been on the rise—literally. These aren't the brazen kind that whine around your ears looking for a landing platform and generally get swatted in the process. These little wretches wait until dark and then furtively search for an exposed patch of skin, especially an ankle or foot. Only female mosquitoes feed on blood, which provides them with the protein necessary for egg production. (Males, which can't even bite, sip flower nectar like innocuous moths.) Using her proboscis, a fine apparatus of six stylets designed for cutting and sucking, she quickly penetrates the skin and probes for a fresh capillary, drawing a full meal before you notice her. The anticoagulant in her saliva causes the allergic reaction that leaves you with an itching knot. Ankle-biters of the worst kind. And she's agile too, usually outmaneuvering your swinging hands and fists.

Tucson's newest mosquitoes are *Aedes aegypti,* a primarily tropical species that prefers urban areas where they find the smallest sources of liquid—from saucers beneath potted plants to forgotten coffee mugs—convenient for reproduction. No one had seen these particular mosquitoes in our area for more than thirty years, and then, in August 1994, a University of Arizona entomologist found several in his backyard. Now, they're in *my* backyard . . . and in my front yard, under my desk, in the bathroom, and in the bedroom.

Karen, naturally, sleeps above the covers, untouched and perfect. I swelter on summer nights beneath damp sheets and still wake with itching, swollen fingers and toes. I could try sleeping with a pig. Folk wisdom claims mosquitoes prefer pigs over people because of the animals' higher body heat. Karen would say it works for her. There must be some truth to that theory about "secretors," people who advertise their blood type through the pores of their skin. A flashing beacon for insects bent on a feast. I must be one, and all the blood-sucking tenants of my neighborhood must be homing in on my scent.

Karen chooses precisely whom she sleeps with. I wish I had that kind of control. All the same, she *is* my human credential, and in this it's possible that I become her human measure. Light is meaningless without darkness. In the same way that beauty has no standard without ugliness, that the gauge of monarch butterflies is stink bugs and cockroaches, my character flaws define Karen. The crawling, sucking denizens of my imperfections distinguish her, if not as impeccable, then at least as beautifully multifaceted. No one is entirely worthless; he can always serve to make someone else look good. It's like when a coworker who's known Karen for years and has come to admire her for her instinctive sense of ethics learns that she is married to a man who spent years in prison. Suddenly there are dimensions to Karen's nature that only an entomologist-turned-sociobiologist like E. O. Wilson could have imagined.

Gizmo won't eat mosquitoes. I've watched him catch lazy flies on warm afternoons and moon-struck moths trapped on my window sill and even an occasional spider eight-legging it across the floor, but he ignores the mosquitoes. Cats for the pack rats that bring the kissing bugs; birds and lizards for the spiders and scorpions . . . so what eats mosquitoes? My solution may finally arouse Karen's interest. I may force her at last to join me in my quirky exasperation over the unwanted, uninvited servants of Beelzebub which beset me.

First, I'll replace the screen on our bedroom window. Next, just before bed, I'll close the door and turn out the lights. Then I'll release the bats.

neutering the boys

The voices started warning me after what happened to the boys. Our two male kittens had begun to act strange—staying out all night, wandering over to the neighbors, stinking up the house. It wasn't normal; something was different about them. Then I caught Gizmo humping Mittens. Bad kitties, I told them and chased them outside. My wife said we needed to "fix" them. *Fix* them? A strange euphemism, I thought, and wondered what part of them she believed was broken. I was reluctant, but Karen called the veterinarian anyway and made the appointment.

Living with four women in the house, I'm severely outnumbered. Even the pet iguana is female. So I felt I had betrayed my sex, carrying the boys to the animal clinic and handing them over to the vet. *(Was it Doctor Balls? No, Bell,* I think.) My wife had sent our daughters to their cousins for a few days. The girls didn't know. This was the detail the voices had warned me about. *Ken,* they said. *The next time your wife sends the kids*

Above: Gizmo

away to the cousins for a few days, you'll be the one with the appointment at the clinic.

At first, I ignored them. Then I had the dream. My wife is standing high in the middle of a crowd of men, her right arm raised above her head. The sky is dark behind her. She looks like Joan of Arc, and it's the look of victory, but there are no flames. From her uplifted fingers dangle a pair of severed testicles.

Karen is not a brutal woman. She would never physically unman anyone regardless of motive. That's too bold for her. Karen is far more subtle, perhaps even a bit devious. Patiently she works her will—a suggestion here, whispered comments there, phone calls to health clinics. In the end she gets her way without bloodying her hands. No more babies, she insists. *You will put all your energy into raising the three daughters you already have.*

A vasectomy is not the same as being neutered. I want to make that clear. It only affects the vas deferens not the testicles, an important distinction. The patient's bloodstream continues to surge with a full dose of undiluted male hormone; like all other men he remains testosterone-impaired. He still retains the essential vehicles for dispersion of his genetic code, even though there's a traffic jam on the off-ramp. Neutering is much more radical. I know. I've seen the five-minute procedure forced upon an unsuspecting, anesthetized cat. First the vet shaves the scrotum and bathes it with antiseptic. Then she makes a quarter-inch incision on the left side and squeezes the sack. Out pops one pink testicle, which she immediately clamps off and snips away. There is very little blood. A second incision on the right side and its twin brother goes into the trash. Once she's tied knots into the loose vas deferens, it's over. No more babies, kittens, that is. Stitches aren't even necessary.

My wife made the appointment at the clinic. Outpatient, virtually painless, one or two days with an ice pack between your legs, no sex for a week, the urologist said during my preliminary visit. Afterward, you shouldn't notice any difference in your sex drive or performance. I read the consent form . . . and re-read the long paragraph of possible complications: "bleeding, infection, sperm granuloma (What is that?), conges-tion, pain, injury or loss of testicle, spontaneous reversal, and increased association with prostate cancer or other health hazards," followed by the list of more common ("serious or possibly fatal") risks like nerve injury, blood clots, heart attack, seizures, and coma. I signed it.

On V day, as the voices had predicted, my daughters went to their cousins again. Karen had arranged for my brother-in-law to pick me up and deliver me to the vet—I mean urologist—wait a couple of hours, then return me home. I wasn't allowed to drive.

The nurses made me nervous. They were all young, attractive—too attractive for urology. I imagined they might be employees at Hooters, the club that shares the same parking lot with the clinic. *Would any be present during the procedure?* I wondered. After Doctor Marks shaved me and bathed me with antiseptic, he began inviting them in. (A knock at the door. Do you mind if she observes? *Yes,* I think. No, I say.) The local anesthetic couldn't numb my embarrassment. For thirty minutes I was vulnerable, exposed; for thirty minutes the source of vulnerability and exposure—and a new quarter-inch incision—was the center of attention. Okay, you never again want to have children, right? Doctor Marks asked when he found the vas deferens. No more babies, I said. One of his assis-tants, a Hispanic woman who had commented on my pink *chones* (wash-ing laundry is still an unfathomable experience for me), supplied the play by play: "Good-bye, vas," she said in turn as Marks snipped and cauter-ized both threads.

After my children came home I hid the ice bag and acted as though nothing had happened. But they were suspicious. It was something in my walk . . . or the way I sat down in slow motion. They remembered coming home to the boys, and something was familiar. Later, Karen told me the girls wanted to know if I had been neutered.

Funny. I try to make distinctions, neutering versus vasectomy, castration versus tube-tying. One reason I write this now, I suppose, is to convince myself that there's no relationship between fathering children and man-hood. It's not working. There's something primal about a man's innate need (impulse?) to win the population contest and cast his seed to the four corners, and something Biblical, too—to be fruitful and multiply. My Catholic fathers (the source of the voices, no doubt), men who believed in large families and raised their boys with this belief, are certainly frowning in their graves. It's hard to fight both nature *and* religion.

So, I've decided not to have my sperm count checked. Maybe there's hope yet. Even now my frustrated tubes might be searching for their loose ends. This isn't wishful thinking. Spontaneous reversal: it could happen. Karen will never know—until it's too late. Until she begins to grow.

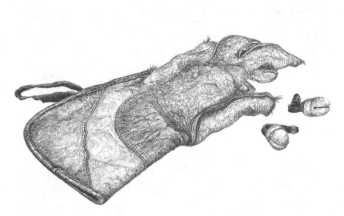

adobe, hawks, and shadows

Dawn at Fairbank, a ghost town on the banks of the San Pedro River in southern Arizona. It's sixty-three degrees, cool compared with the mornings I'm used to in a desert that shrugs off these temperatures long before July. I stick my head into a worn adobe building still labeled Post Office, but it's quiet and dark inside. Deserted. Beyond this, several empty, sad foundations mark the places where other adobes have already bled back to dirt.

Loneliness is here, expressed in the absence of something vital, and I cannot deny the fact that it affects me. Somehow it reflects my own inadequacies: a blown career, abused and discarded relationships, one of them with a best friend. But I cover this well with activity, just as mesquite and feral walnut trees now obscure the old town site. Even the birds migrate, leave home.

Birds. Fairbank definitely is a place for birds. Perhaps it's because of the

---

Above: Falconer's glove and bells

feeders and nest boxes someone has placed among the mesquite or the oozing water spigot with its algae rime. I spot ash-throated flycatchers, calling with plaintive voices, and western tanagers in bright, sunburst colors, along with the ubiquitous mourning doves and obnoxious Gila woodpeckers. Gambel's quail complain from the undergrowth while swallows swirl the air overhead. Vermilion flycatchers, however, demand my attention. They flit from branch to branch, bright scraps of holiday ribbon, snapping at insects as they show off their aerobatic skills with precise wings. I watch them, enchanted by the absolutely natural way they command their element. They could easily trespass fences and razor wire.

But as tempting as it is, I haven't come to Fairbank to be charmed by songbirds. Fairbank is just a beginning, like the train depot it once was to those traveling to and from Tombstone, a stepping off place. I've come here, to this part of the San Pedro Riparian National Conservation Area, for something a little more elusive—gray hawks. Nesting gray hawks. Rumors of a nesting pair in a cottonwood gallery south of Fairbank have been circulating among bird watchers for the past few weeks back in Tucson. I've never seen one, and I'm hoping to add this species, one of the rarest raptors in the United States, to my life list. That growing catalogue of birds is my newest pride, my favorite topic of discussion. Lately, it's been my singular purpose; today, it's an obsession.

There was a time when I shared my enthusiasm for birds with children. I couldn't help it. Since the day I moved to the desert at age nine, birds have fascinated me—their songs, the weave of their nests, the hue of their eggs. As a result, they became an important part of my life science curriculum in the public school where I taught. I took my students on field trips to aviaries and required them to memorize color slides of common songbirds before traveling to remote regions on overnight birding trips. Together we called great horned and pygmy and screech owls on moonless nights with the owls' own recorded voices. As a falconer, I brought living, hunting raptors into my classroom, and as a taxidermist, I salvaged their dead bodies from highways to preserve as study specimens of feathered structure and form. We learned about the aerodynamics of pelican wings and the silencing effect of an owl wing's leading edge. And not just birds, but my enthusiasm for all life spilled over into my teaching. My classroom became a menagerie of living, breathing creatures: marine and freshwater fish, toads and salamanders, rattlesnakes and boa constrictors, mice and hamsters and Guinea pigs (the latter mostly to feed the snakes). My whole life, not just the bird-watcher in me, was in those display cases and aquariums and animals and study mounts and books and charts . . . and students. Part of it is still there.

My wife thinks this whole birder thing is ridiculous, but she humors me as she has with all my expensive hobbies. Scuba diving, fish keeping, falconry, hunting and fishing, taxidermy—she's tolerated them all, outlasting my enthusiasm. Now that I no longer teach, no longer work at all, actually, since my release from prison, my hobbies excuse me from making a career of domestic chores. I tell Karen, the practical, more sensible one in the marriage, that I can earn a living by writing for magazines about my wilderness excursions, a good use of my presently worthless biology degree. Weekend birding, with only a pair of binoculars, a knapsack of field guides, and a tank of gas, can provide for us during this latest hump in my life, I explain. She hangs onto her job, her security. She's not convinced.

The books say the gray hawk is a medium-sized predator whose most distinguishing feature is, not surprisingly, its grayness. Its head and back are solid ash gray and fine lines of the color bar its breast. The only other easily recognizable trait is the bird's white rump patch and black- and white-banded tail. The small, short-winged hawk isn't like other soaring hawks, however. It flies by darting in short bursts with rapid wing beats and hunts by perching for long periods in thick foliage before ambushing its prey. Because it behaves in this way like a goshawk, it's sometimes called the Mexican goshawk. Some people even suggest placing the gray hawk in a separate classification altogether, one where its uniqueness isn't blurred by the more common and ordinary raptors.

Gray hawks range in scattered places throughout Mexico, Central

America, and as far south as Argentina. Fortunately for my wife's pocketbook, the Southwest is the northernmost limit of their range, and it is here, along a few rivers in southeastern Arizona, that a small number of the hawks come in the summer to breed. In fact, according to my library research, most gray hawk nests in the United States are found in Arizona, where scientists have counted more than fifty-five pairs along the Santa Cruz and San Pedro drainages.

Historically, gray hawks probably centered on the riparian galleries of the Santa Cruz River. In 1937, ornithologist A. C. Bent found them "quite common" along the river near Tucson, and until the 1960s, they nested along Tucson's Rillito River and Tanque Verde Creek. Now, because of the massive cuttings of mesquite, hackberry, and cottonwood trees that fueled southeastern Arizona's early economy, the hawks have retreated from much of the Santa Cruz to the San Pedro floodplain. Here, where I'm standing today, one-third of the gray hawks known to breed in Arizona—in the United States for that matter—are nesting along this thin riparian corridor.

From Fairbank, a dirt road leads me south, where it runs parallel to the Southern Pacific Railroad. A quarter mile farther west beyond the tracks, huge broccoli-like cottonwoods trace the course of the San Pedro. After fifteen minutes of walking, passing only a pair of turkey vultures soaking the morning sun into black, outstretched wings above an old wooden trestle, I spot a suspicious silhouette on a lower branch of one of the cottonwoods. Is this it? My heart thumps, and I feel a familiar shortness of breath.

I decide to forsake the road and bushwhack to the river but soon discover that wearing shorts is a mistake. Immediately across the tracks, saltbushes barricade the sandy floodplain, constantly forcing me to change directions and backtrack. Every lead seems to run out, and I must find another, only to be thwarted again. Frustrated, I begin pushing through anyway, stomp-navigating the thickets. I might as well wear a blindfold. The hard, dry branches clutch at my legs and leave me with angry welts as punishment for trespassing. A quarter mile stroll turns into a half-mile, bloody, sacrificial march, particularly as I enter the thorn-tedious mesquite bosque. And still the river is no closer.

When I look for it, the hawk is gone. My wanderings among these worthless shrubs have flushed it from its perch. Just as I'm ready to give up, I stumble upon an odd-looking elevated berm and climb to higher ground. The earthwork is unnaturally straight and narrow; dark, broken rocks bloom in places along its crest. It appears to be a railway without ties or steel, and I guess it's an abandoned section of the New Mexico and Arizona Railroad that gave birth to Fairbank in 1882. Above the thorns now, I follow it to the concrete abutment of a long-dismantled bridge and the dry San Pedro River.

From my vantage fifty feet above the sand, I can see that the drainage cuts through the desert, tearing at it on both flanks. There's no water, but everywhere are signs of flood—high banks with hanging tree roots, twisted vegetation, great river-worn boulders. In places where both water and earth have relaxed, cottonwoods tower skyward above understories of willow and ash. These islands of green are what I'm looking for, nesting habitat for gray hawks.

Supposedly, the hawks have been courting and nesting since their arrival in April. My field guides tell me that a nesting pair becomes extremely vocal, each bird calling out to the other with loud, repeated screeches. I listen, but I hear only mourning doves. I hike south, "upstream" in the sand. The air under the cottonwoods smells like the inside of a damp adobe dwelling, and their shade feels like it's cooling my skin by at least ten degrees. I search the trees, one after another, until my legs are weak from walking on soft ground. I find no nests. Even the doves hide from me. The only things that fly around here are gnats. The tiny black beggars whine incessantly. Still frustrated, I begin to doubt my original sighting. Maybe it was a raven. The stinking greasy scavengers are everywhere. I have a personal bias against ravens. They always remind me of where I've spent the last eight years of my life. Daily I would see them, black and buzzardlike, croaking and squabbling over the trash dumpsters just outside the prison fence.

Despite the hawks' absence, the area seems a perfect place for them.

The bosque gives them a territory where they can hunt whiptail lizards and other reptiles, their favorite prey. The riparian trees make for high, secure nests. So where are they? I wonder where I went wrong, if I should have stayed on the road. This early in July I was counting on being able to locate a nest with fledglings.

I avoid the mesquite and saltbush thickets by allowing the San Pedro to take me back to Fairbank. On the way I notice some spattered white-wash in the leaf litter under a cottonwood. It's chalky and dry, but unmistakably the droppings of a hawk. This is a good sign: a recently occupied nest for sure. I back away from the tree and peer into its upper branches. The nest is there, tucked into a high fork and nearly concealed in the leaves. But it's empty. Abandoned.

Back at Fairbank I peel an orange under a mesquite and watch the fly-catchers. The silly playfulness of the birds eases my disappointment. While I'm eating, a huge woman extracts herself from one of the tiny Bureau of Land Management (BLM) trailers and approaches me. Her name is Kris, and she tells me in a voice that would frighten wildlife for miles that the BLM pays her a small stipend to live here and watch over the place, which means mostly picking up tourist trash and answering their questions. I tell her I'm looking for gray hawks; she's not surprised. And she doesn't hide her disdain. People have been coming down here for weeks, she says, just to see one nesting pair. They're gone. Can't handle the traffic.

I learn from her that Rich Glinsky, a wildlife specialist with the Arizona Game and Fish, has been studying gray hawks on the San Pedro for years. As far back as 1986 he was warning people that the nesting birds can't tolerate human disturbance. Even small numbers of people can cause nest abandonment.

Joseph Wood Krutch was right when he wrote: "When all the 'collecting,' photographing, and experimentation is taken into consideration—the best friend of the birds is often the one who pays no attention to them." First we cut down their trees. Then poison them with DDT and shoot them as pests and for sport. Today, more wise for the experience, we love them to death. Why is it that even the footprints we leave behind cause harm? Why must human culture always have an impact? And here I am, just as guilty as the developers and tourists. Checking birds off as if they were items on a shopping list. Teacher, bird watcher, writer—but still a *consumer* in the end. Seems I can't escape my own greedy human nature. Am I fooling myself? Wanting to be a naturalist and writer? I failed at teaching before I'd given it five years and wasted twice that many years since then. I'm almost forty. Maybe I should go back to hanging laundry and keeping house. The gray hawks, at least, would fare better.

I spend the rest of the afternoon poking around the ruins at Fairbank. Not much remains of the town that, in the 1880s, grew up around a Wells Fargo office and train depot, a hotel and three restaurants, four stores, and most importantly, five saloons. The Montezuma Hotel, according to some courtesy information I find in a steel box, lies buried under the highway. One adobe, the Commercial Company (once a general store, post office, and saloon—for convenience sake?) seems intact after its recent refitting by the BLM. I look into one of the houses behind it. It's dark and musty, a jumbled mess of old furniture and appliances.

Fairbank is too close to the highway. Easy access to it over the years means there's nothing much left. Seven historic buildings, two of them outhouses, are all that remain of a town that outlasted most others in the area—Millville, Contention City, Charleston—surviving busted silver mines, floods, and even an earthquake. Fairbank is more than dead and buried. It's a looted tomb.

I've seen Charleston, and there is a difference. No road takes you there. Hidden among the mesquite, Charleston has rested peacefully for more than a hundred years, decaying naturally in its own unmarked grave on the banks of the San Pedro. When I visited the ghost town with Richard Shelton, an author and teacher and probably one of the few people who knows its location, the river was flowing. I could smell its green pungency even before I could see it. It wasn't deep, and its current was sluggish, but there was water.

We picked our way along the river's edge, my wife and I following

Richard as he shared with us stories about his first encounter with Charleston. Karen had read aloud from his book, *Going Back to Bisbee,* about Fairbank, Charleston, and Tombstone—the whole region—during the ride down from Tucson. "I knew I'd found it before I saw anything," he told us. "I could feel something . . . and it scared me."

The riparian corridor seemed tamer there; high banks still prevail, but they are less ravaged by flood and more overgrown with cottonwood and willow. Near Charleston, the river is a narrow, verdant strip, but the desert encroaches, slipping furtive fingers right down to the water in places. I expected to see vermilion flycatchers and black phoebes, minnows darting for cover in two inches of water, and thumb-sized toads skipping across the wet sand—creatures common to the river. But I didn't find any of these. Only tracks, raccoon, I think, in the mud. The river was silent.

After a mile or so, Richard took us into the mesquite on the west side of the river. Then, after a few moments, he stopped. I blinked. An eight-foot adobe wall had materialized as if the trees had shifted slightly to reveal it to us. It was some kind of gift. We crept toward it, and another wall followed the first and then more, until there were rows of them, some ten or twelve feet high with corners and doorways and windows, every one crowded by mesquite. It seemed as though the trees had thrown protective arms and hands and fingers around the melting adobe as if to hold it together just a little longer. The twisted and heavy trees, as the only children of this place, had grown up to become guardians of their elders. I felt privileged to be there.

Fairbank can't compare to Charleston. Its Presence is gone, replaced by cheerful birds and loud caretakers. Scraped to the ground or refurbished with fresh adobe and white plaster, Fairbank is on its way to being another tourist-hungry Tombstone. (Today, actors dressed as cowboys rob the tourist train with much fanfare and bravado.) There are no more discoveries to be made there. No one wonders about the lives of the people who passed conversation between barstools or delivered word from home or taught grammar and spelling to miners' kids, people without names and faces whose only legacy is what they left to their children. Eternal things like ideas and character. Adobe and mesquite. Charleston.

I stand next to the remains of Fairbank's schoolhouse. It's not as old as the town, and it wasn't made of adobe but Permastone, the gypsum quarried in another part of the state. Still, I find that there is something lingering here—more so in this spot than in all of Fairbank. I imagine I hear thick pencils dragging on paper and covert whispering. A teacher has his back to the class. He's working furiously at the chalkboard on the drawing of an insect . . . or a bird. Perhaps it's a hawk. And then I begin to realize how my writing about gray hawks does have merit. It has value for those who don't care to come looking for them, but who care about the birds all the same. Care enough, possibly, to fight to protect this narrow, tree-rimmed spoke of river. Gray hawks on the page may inspire people to become more concerned about diminishing places, to pay more attention to conservation issues, to support organizations and programs involved with preserving critical habitat like biological corridors. For gray hawks. And also for leopard frogs and mud turtles, Gila topminnows and ringneck snakes. And for people. The Nature Conservancy comes to mind. And the controversial Sonoran Desert Conservation Plan, only recently getting attention.

And I could do better. To begin with, I could abandon my arrogance. I could change my attitude, stop "hunting" the birds, any birds, and learn to tread more lightly. I was a teacher for five years, and I forfeited that privilege. Instead, by default it seems, I chase birds. But isn't being a teacher more than a profession? More than a choice of career? Like being a husband or father. Writing about nature isn't just another way to occupy my time. It's an expression of my need to share with others things that are important to me, to leave behind something lasting. To make a difference. Teaching was never what I did, I know that now. It was who I was . . . who I am.

As I stand next to the school's ruins, something feels familiar. I sense my place here. I see the figure at the chalkboard dusting the chalk from his hands and turning toward the class. I see my own face.

author's note

I learned of the Appellate Court's decision to return me to prison as I was finishing the first draft of this last essay, "Adobe, Hawks, and Shadows." It was Thanksgiving, 1995, and I had recently enrolled in the creative writing program at the University of Arizona. Richard Shelton was teaching "Literature of the Southwest" and taking graduate students to places like Fairbank and Charleston on the San Pedro River in southeast Arizona. Our visit that fall inspired me to write about the gray hawks of the area, and I would return there several more times before I went back to prison the following summer of 1996.

Above: Gray hawk feather

ABOUT THE AUTHOR

When Ken Lamberton published his first creative nonfiction book *Wilderness and Razor Wire* (Mercury House, 2000), the *San Francisco Chronicle* called it, ". . . entirely original: an edgy, ferocious, subtly complex collection of essays. . . ." The book won the 2002 John Burroughs Medal for outstanding nature writing. He has published more than a hundred science and nature articles in many national magazines, and his essays have appeared in literary journals like *Manoa, Northern Lights, Alligator Juniper, Puerto Del Sol, The Gettysburg Review,* and David Quammen's anthology *The Best American Science and Nature Writing 2000.* His second book, *Chiricahua Mountains: Bridging the Borders of Wildness,* was published in October 2003 by the University of Arizona Press. He holds degrees in biology and creative writing from the University of Arizona and lives with his wife and daughters in Tucson.